Praise for *Step Up*

"*Step Up* is an empowering and mobilizing call to action, full of emotional and incredibly relevant storytelling. With a compelling blend of innovative research and personal stories, Ash Beckham has created an artful and visionary guide to stepping up in all areas of your life and becoming a more inclusive, active, and confident version of yourself. Through the foundational eight pillars of leadership, *Step Up* shows readers that everyone has the potential (and responsibility) to speak up for themselves and others, and that we all have the capabilities and stories necessary to become better leaders."

JENNIFER BROWN
founder, president, and CEO of Jennifer Brown Consulting;
author of *Inclusion* and *How to Be an Inclusive Leader*

"This book is every bit as impactful as watching Ash Beckham share her story onstage in a packed auditorium. There, as here, her vibrant, wide-open heart shines through. *Step Up* is more valuable than any 'inclusion workshop' I've ever attended. Ash knows firsthand that the way to broaden our perspective about difference and unseat our unconscious habits is not by top-down command but by grassroots understanding. *Step Up* not only imparts that understanding by blending storytelling, inspiration, and science, it also offers actionable homework. It's a book. It's a workshop. It's a motivational ideal for all of us who aspire to be better, kinder versions of ourselves."

SUE HEILBRONNER
CEO of MergeLane Fund

"Ash's insights jump off the pages of this incredibly compelling read! Her personal stories made me laugh, cry, and, most importantly, relate. I would recommend this book to interns, CEOs, and everyone in between. Ash's one-of-a-kind take on leadership is the fresh perspective we need in today's world."

ERIN URITUS
CEO of Out & Equal Workplace Advocates

"Ash Beckham somehow created a self-improvement book that is neither boring nor pretentious! She took on a topic that people can relate to in everyday life—how to become a better leader—and infused it with humor, emotion, and practical tips I will actually use because they're not overly complicated or annoying. I often forget that leadership transcends the workplace, and the more I can include this mind-set in my everyday life, the better person I will be for myself, others, and the world around me. My favorite (and toughest) challenge is to practice patience as it relates to leadership. Ash reminds us that sometimes being a leader is to do the opposite of what you think you should. Thank you, Ash, for sharing yourself and this gift with the world!"

NICOLE DEBOOM
founder and CEO of Skirt Sports, Inc.

ASH BECKHAM

STEP UP

How to Live with Courage and Become an Everyday Leader

sounds true
BOULDER, COLORADO

Sounds True
Boulder, CO 80306

Published 2020

Cover design by Jennifer Miles
Book design by Beth Skelley

Printed in Canada

Library of Congress Cataloging-in-Publication Data

Names: Beckham, Ash, author.
Title: Step Up: How to Live with Courage
    and Become an Everyday Leader / Ash Beckham.
Description: Boulder, CO : Sounds True, [2020] | Identifiers: LCCN
2019025252 (print) | LCCN 2019025253 (ebook) |
    ISBN 9781683642787 (hardcover) | ISBN 9781683643173 (ebook)
Subjects: LCSH: Leadership. | Social change. | Courage.
Classification: LCC BF637.L4 B363 2020 (print) | LCC BF637.L4 (ebook) |
    DDC 158/.4--dc23
LC record available at https://lccn.loc.gov/2019025252
LC ebook record available at https://lccn.loc.gov/2019025253

10 9 8 7 6 5 4 3 2 1

To Dad,
my hero, my coach, and my inspiration.
I miss you every day.

CONTENTS

INTRODUCTION

EACH EVERYDAY LEADER HAS A STARTING POINT— HERE'S MINE

When I have to state my job title, I usually say "accidental advocate." Speaking and activism are what I'm known for today. But for the longest time, I had no idea this was what I was going to do with my life.

In 2010, I was happily living in Boulder, Colorado. I owned a couple of small businesses, and I had an amazing circle of friends. The nature of my work as an entrepreneur gave me the freedom to return home to Ohio to visit family whenever I wanted. To paraphrase the T-shirts, life was good! My activism was just being myself—a shaved-headed, small-business-owning lesbian. I lived in a community that was safe for the most part. If I stayed in my lane, I didn't ruffle any feathers. Everyone was happy. I had achieved acceptance. That was the finish line I had been striving to cross. I was there. I had won the race, or at least I'd had a respectable finish.

Then, suddenly, a lot of kids came into my life. I did not have kids of my own yet, but the people I loved all started having babies — my sister and friends who were as close as family. I suddenly realized then that my sexuality and nonconforming gender expression (shaved head, baggy cargo shorts, etc.) affected more people than just me: at some point these kids were going to run into a challenge or a conflict because they loved me and because I was gay. Someone would say something in a hallway or a locker room that would be intentionally or unintentionally derogatory to gay people. And then these kids would be torn between what they had always known and this new (to them) tiered paradigm. I realized that despite my comfortable life and security in my identity, I had a responsibility to be part of cultural change. I needed to step up. It was my first inkling that I needed to attempt to make the world a better place. I wanted these kids (and everyone, for that matter) to love whoever they loved without having to worry about defending them. I knew — from experience — that just because people were different did not also mean they were dangerous.

Everyone has their own way of stepping up. To be the most effective, our methods of stepping up must be genuine. For me it wasn't about protests or policy change or guilting people into changing their behavior. I had yelled and screamed and soapboxed to no avail. For me, it was critical to engage with folks who were allies-in-waiting. My second hometown of Boulder, Colorado, is a liberal place, so it seemed like a good place to start. The conversation about marriage equality, for example, was moot; almost everyone was for it. But how do you get the good-hearted folks you see every day to make changes to their own *behavior*? I knew that resting on progressive political stances was not enough. Cultural change happens at a grassroots level, with small, intentional adjustments to how we live, how we act, and how we interact. It was that kind of change I wanted to inspire in people. I realized that I needed to lead not with the loudest voice but with the biggest heart.

My journey as an advocate started with a talk I gave at an Ignite Boulder event in February 2013, called "Eliminating 'Gay' as a Pejorative from our Lexicon." I was simply trying to get people to understand that their words make an impact on others. The talk quickly got traction online and shifted the course of my life permanently. We don't necessarily pick when we become leaders; sometimes our lives morph into a path of leadership. Since then, I have spoken in classrooms, ballrooms, and boardrooms around the world. My online talks currently have more than 15 million views. I have spoken at LGBTQ community centers with five people in the room and at Fortune 100 sales meetings with thousands of people in the room. The message is the same: before you look out, look in. Listen before you yell. Find humor in our shared experiences. Focus on our common goal of a better world, not on our differences. Don't start with politics or policy, start with human connection. We all have the capacity to be leaders in our own way; we just need to be brave enough to take action, to separate ourselves from the pack and change our own behavior first.

When I started speaking publicly, I ran into a fair amount of resistance. Not with the message — people were inspired by my story. I started to lose them when I suggested that we could all be leaders. *Now it's your turn. Find your own path and blaze it.* When they heard this message, people started to shut down. Some could never see themselves stepping up in the way I had. Overwhelmingly, the reason people did not believe they could fully be themselves is that they feared the repercussions and judgments that would come if they were truly authentic to their voice and their values.

For the first few years, I accepted that response. To fully be ourselves in the world takes a tremendous amount of courage. I just needed to find the people who had this courage and inspire them. But then I kept meeting folks who were already incredible leaders. They were making change happen in their companies and in their communities but they were afraid to assign themselves the label of "leader." I wanted to find out what was driving all of this fear. Was it something people could overcome? Could we eliminate it?

The challenge is that as creatures of habit, we get into ruts. These ruts can be physical, emotional, or psychological. If we take the same way to work every day and mindlessly follow the route on autopilot, that is a rut. If we do the same routine at the gym every day, that is a rut. If we find ourselves continuously unwilling to stand up against microaggressions that we see happening around us, that is a rut.

We can also view ourselves in very fixed ways. We cannot imagine being a leader, even in an everyday kind of way. We can't envision ourselves with the courage to push our comfort zones. Anything that is a habitual pattern of behavior or thinking that has the sole justification of "that's the way it's always been" is a rut. But as we begin to step up, that justification does not work anymore. Why would we hold ourselves back?

We all have ruts that we don't even think about. Let me show you right now.

Sit back and fold your arms. Really—do this. Now, uncross them and recross them with the other arm on top. Feels different, yes? You just broke through an ingrained habit. That is what it feels like. The only reason the second way feels uncomfortable is because you have always done it in the other direction. For me, I put my left arm on top. When I put the right arm on top the first few times, I had to switch immediately. Something felt wrong and unnatural. But the more I crossed them the less habitual way, the more comfortable I became with that way, too. Now I don't even think twice about which way I cross my arms. Both feel natural. That is the beauty of our brains— they have neuroplasticity, the ability to make new pathways.

We often don't try to change simply because it feels so much easier to do things as we have always done them. Doing things differently means facing the unknown. But we *can* change. And it can feel really good—or at least interesting. Habits can be broken.

Sometimes, the biggest fear holding us back is the fear that we do not have the right or the ability to hold any kind of leadership role. We second-guess ourselves: *Who the hell do you think you are? Why would anyone listen to you? You are just a stay-at-home mom or a twenty-year-old or a middle manager, and anyway, your GPA was average* and so on — fill in the blank. We focus on our perceived shortcomings rather than seeing our personal experiences as things that give us relatability and expertise.

We are leaders in our lives by how we show up in the world every day. That means how we interact at the grocery store or at our kid's soccer game or with our partner or in our jobs. Leadership is not a position but rather a *disposition*. It does not require a staff or a specific salary.

Everyone has the uniqueness required to become an everyday leader because it's about the kinds of decisions we make in ordinary (and sometimes not-so-ordinary) situations. As we make higher choices over and over again, choosing the harder right over the easier wrong — or over indifference — we make an impact. Every day and day after day. The side benefit of our actions is that we show the way for other people to step up to their conscious choices and actions as well if they so choose.

How to Use This Book

Currently, our world is ultradivisive. We need everyday leaders to step up and be the change they wish to see in the world. Anyone can do it. You can do it.

Throughout this book, we will look at eight pillars of everyday leadership — empathy, responsibility, courage, grace, individuality, humility, patience, and authenticity.

These pillars are not isolated from each other. They are meant as skills to be practiced together in an intermingled, integrated way. Sometimes we use one just to give us the opportunity to use another: practicing humility gives us courage; practicing empathy leads us to responsibility, and so on. When we are comfortable embracing all of these skills and traits, we can enter any situation with confidence. The pillars are simple, approachable, and universal. When we practice them in our daily lives, we also become an example to others.

Embracing the eight pillars of everyday leadership allows us to commit to self-awareness and self-accountability in all our actions and decisions. There's no situation too big or too small for us. We always have the opportunity to show up fully. This commitment empowers us to be more ourselves rather than less and to be more of ourselves more of the time. We embrace the precepts of everyday leadership internally, and then we begin to see these values flourish in our lives externally. I show you all of this in action in the book with lots of personal stories of successes and failures. My hope is that you walk away from every chapter feeling inspired and with concrete actions that you can implement right away.

It is my deepest wish that all of us find the courage to step up, speak out, and become everyday leaders in our own lives. To be fully transparent, I still have fear in putting my stories out into the world. The doubts come quickly and often. Will this book resonate with readers? Is it strong enough to handle the criticism that will inevitably come? Am I? But that is what the path to every-day leadership is all about: having the courage to face our fears and take action, because the potential for greater good outweighs the personal risk. My hope is not that this book gives you the answers. I certainly don't have them all. My hope is that this book gives you the tools to craft your own solutions, to define and then embrace what everyday leadership looks like to you.

Let's roll up our sleeves and get started.

PILLAR 1

··

EMPATHY

··

Understanding Someone Else's "Why"

As everyday leaders, we accept that the only thing we can control is how we act in the world around us. With this acceptance we develop the courage to step up in situations that other people might shy away from out of uncertainty or fear. These are often the same situations we ourselves have avoided in the past. Because it's much easier to do nothing. In fact, most of us go through a time of doing nothing. It takes empathy, patience, courage—and a sense of responsibility and humility—to do *something*. In this way, everyday leaders separate themselves from the pack. That's what this book is about.

Empathy is foundational to anyone who wants to make a difference, no matter how big or how small. It might not be the first quality that springs to mind when we think of leadership, but it should be *our* starting point.

Empathy is different from sympathy or compassion, and everyday leaders are different from conventional corporate or political leaders. Empathy does not mean "feeling for" another but rather "coming to understand" another. For everyday leaders, the more we empathize, the greater our ability to connect and collaborate for the greater good.

Think for a moment of someone whose opinion on some topic is opposite to yours. Conversations with this person tend to go downhill fast. You know this person, right? Maybe you have more than one of them in your life. We are so attached to our opinions that we refuse to even acknowledge this person's different perspective — and if they do acknowledge ours, it's likely we don't even hear them. As soon as they open their mouth, we are already resisting them. We don't even think about it. We take a position, and we stick to it. One of us is right and one of us is wrong. We get into a familiar us-versus-them paradigm right away. We may even disagree with no knowledge of what they are talking about because our default position is to disagree with them.

But what if we were willing to *understand* this person's perspective, no matter what it was? What if we approached the conversation as an opportunity to learn how someone else sees things rather than as an opportunity to change their mind or to defend our position? What would happen if we listened even though we also disagreed? What would we lose? This paradigm embraces "we." There are no sides, no right and wrong, just different perspectives.

For me, this concept of listening without judgment became apparent during the 2016 U.S. presidential election. My family owns a girls' fastpitch softball tournament company, and through this work, I have close relationships with the people who run a privately owned softball park in Parkersburg, West Virginia. I never assumed that I would share the same political views with the owners or the staff: I am a lesbian from a progressive town in Colorado, while these guys are blue collar, born and raised in rural West Virginia. I was likely the only lesbian they knew. Out of respect for each other, we avoided politics, and our relationship worked. We genuinely liked each other. But when the *Access Hollywood* tapes came out showing the then-presidential candidate, Donald Trump, bragging about sexually assaulting women, I assumed anyone involved in girls' sports would not vote for him. What were we teaching our girls if we put our vote behind someone accused of repeated sexual harassment? Or someone who acted like a bully or made racist comments? To me, these things are in direct opposition to the principles of teamwork and egalitarianism that sports were meant to teach.

But then I had a conversation. Typically, I stay away from politics in the softball business, but while raking the fields with some of the field maintenance crew, I let out some of my frustration with Trump. There was an awkward silence in which I realized that I had miscalculated where the crew stood on this candidate.

Then one of the guys spoke up, "I don't like what he says either. He is certainly not someone I want as a role model for my kids. But I have been working odd jobs for the last five years since the factory closed. There are no jobs here." He told me that he used to believe he could pay for his kids' college education, but these days he was just hoping they could get through high school before he lost the family home.

"So, yeah, he's a jerk. He says racist and homophobic things I do not agree with. You know how I feel about that stuff; I adore you and your wife. You are family. But he is the only one talking about bringing jobs back." This guy felt that Trump was the only candidate who was addressing his baseline concerns.

"I don't care if Satan himself was running, I would vote for him if I thought he would help us around here."

With that, everyone went back to raking the field.

This man's honesty and vulnerability blew me away. He was not voting for Trump because of what Trump said but *in spite* of it. He had even more urgent priorities than a good model for his kids. He needed to provide for his family. This superseded his disgust.

When I understood his perspective, I began to see why some folks considered those people voting for Hillary Clinton elitists. The fact that day-to-day survival was not my number-one priority was a privilege. I didn't need to worry about keeping my house or the economic viability of my town. My livelihood was not directly linked to the profit-and-loss statement of a large corporation. I was financially secure, I lived in an economically diverse state, and I was college educated. I had the luxury of judging the candidates based on my opinion of their character and positions on social policy rather than having to ignore behavior that offended me because of the promise of having my basic needs covered. I certainly don't see myself as an elitist, but I could understand why people might have seen me as one.

After hearing the field maintenance guy — and really listening to where he was coming from — I started to view people who voted for Trump differently. I learned one man's *why*, and my entire line of thinking about half the country flipped. It became irrelevant whether or not I thought jobs were *actually* going to come back, as Trump promised. In an instant, I saw that my own assumptions were just as toxic as the stereotypes about me that I fought every day. I was a gender-nonconforming lesbian, so people often assumed that I was a gym teacher and that I hated men. Neither was true. I also did not own a Subaru, nor did I have a dozen cats. I knew what it was like to be stereotyped, and yet there I was assuming things about this man in West Virginia and, by extension, half of the country that voted differently than I did.

Here's the thing: Just listening to another person's perspective does not give us empathy. We need to listen *without judgment*. We have to stay open. This is key, and for most adults, it's not easy to do. I'll say it again: empathy requires only that we *understand*, not *agree with* someone else. Judgment clouds our objectivity and limits our ability to connect. If all I do is see a situation through my own familiar lens, I will inevitably pass judgment on other people instead of genuinely listening to them. I would have seen my colleague on the softball field as a misogynistic racist, just like the person he was voting for. And that would have blocked me from seeing where he was coming from and understanding his real concerns. If he had simply told me that he was voting for Trump, it would have reinforced my stereotypes. But when he told me *why* he was voting for Trump, it shattered those stereotypes.

This is really important. If we're striving for inclusiveness and diversity — to give everyone a seat at the table — then we need to understand the "why" of each individual. This allows us to relate to a lot more people and for everyone to feel heard. Because, in reality, people will not always agree. The best groups and organizations incorporate many different perspectives, and with difference also comes disagreement. When differences inevitably come up, we are able to acknowledge each perspective and proceed with the best course of action for all. We might not implement the strategy that each individual proposes, but at least everyone gets heard and feels respected.

We must avoid writing people off. I had been friends with the field maintenance guy for years. I gave his kids piggyback rides. I'd often cracked open a beer with him in the parking lot at the end of the day. This guy was the first of the bunch to congratulate me when I proposed to my wife. He was an ally, but more importantly, he was a friend. Did this one difference of opinion destroy all of that? Were years of connection and the countless things we had in common erased because we filled out our ballots differently?

I believe that most of us are rational humans who want to pursue life, liberty, and happiness. When we write people off because they don't quite conform to our values, we are excluding people who we want and need at the table, people we can learn from and people we can teach. We cannot claim to be inclusive if we leave people behind so hastily. What if we saw everyone as a potential ally? What if our first thought was not how someone might offend us but rather how they might support us? Or, better yet, how we might support them? Despite the vitriol with which some U.S. voters refer to one another, the vast majority of us are not on the extreme left or right but in the middle. The fringe elements comprise only about 10 percent of the population. That leaves 80 percent of us who are not extremists. That gives us lots of opportunities to find common ground.

One place where it may seem counterintuitive to strive to understand the other side is in the military. We expect the army's leadership style to be the traditional "us above all else" one, a perfect example of the us-versus-them paradigm. After all, we want our side to win. The safety of troops and civilians and the success of our missions rely on making ourselves our top priority. But, in fact, the U.S. Army Field Manuals, which contain key information for military procedures and survival in the field, cover empathy as a leadership skill. Surprised? So was I.

One officer, Lieutenant Colonel Kevin Cutright, wrote an extended essay, "Empathy for Carnivores," that gives more thought to the issue. The paper encourages the military to put empathy into action rather than paying it lip service. The quality is already listed as something that officers need when relating to soldiers and when planning strategies during conflict. The manual acknowledges that officers are more successful when they understand the people they are interacting with, both within the U.S. Army and in the places where they are stationed. But, Cutright says, it could be made better use of. When empathy is properly understood and implemented, it improves our thinking, both creatively and critically. In the military, it improves campaign designs as well as assessments of how campaigns went. It's not only about having good character. It's also about being a better leader.

He also makes an important distinction for those people who get hung up on empathy being a "soft skill" that has no place in the military. He says, "Empathy may result in sympathy, but the two concepts are distinct. Empathy involves only understanding another's perspective; it does not require agreeing with that perspective."

To me, Cutright's understanding of empathy is empowering. When we know that understanding does not require agreeing, then we can listen to *anything*. We can truly understand the *why* behind the actions of others without ever condoning those actions. If we can practice empathy regularly, there are very few people in the world who we can't at least understand. If military officers can use empathy in planning combat or carrying out a campaign, certainly we can employ it in our everyday lives as well.

But empathy is not something we can understand simply by reading about it or by taking it as a position. It's not theoretical. We need to feel its impact to fully comprehend its power.

One of my first big lessons in empathy happened at my sister's wedding back in 2004. I'd been living happily in Colorado for almost a decade, where I was fully out and fully a part of the community there. When I'd left Ohio, I'd had the sole purpose of "finding myself." What I hadn't known then was that finding myself would mean coming out as gay.

My little sister's wedding would be the first time I'd be seeing a lot of extended family and friends from the community I'd grown up in. Knowing Mandy, I knew it was not going to be an ordinary wedding. It would be a 500-person, midwestern extravaganza held in a huge hotel ballroom, and it would be the social event of the spring in Toledo, Ohio. Sure enough, my sister labored over every detail. Each place setting had multiple forks. I swear nearly everyone we had ever met, from kindergarten to college, was in the room. That included people I'd known my whole life, too.

I was thrilled for my sister, but I had some trepidation about attending this huge event in my hometown. My larger family had responded in a variety of ways to my coming out, and those responses ranged from accepting to neutral to unknown. My closest family was incredibly supportive, but there would be other folks at the wedding whom I hadn't seen in years. They knew I was gay, of course, because news in all hometowns travels fast. But hearing the news and interacting with me in person were two different things. I didn't necessarily expect a warm welcome from everyone. Also, there would be an open bar, so really, anything could happen.

With the full support of my immediate family, my girlfriend attended the wedding with me. My sister also extended a few extra invites to me so my table would be full of friends, most of whom were gay too. I knew I'd have a safe place to land no matter how the evening played out.

My sister had asked me to be the maid of honor, and I'd accepted. I conceded to wearing a dress, even though I typically prefer men's jeans and button-downs. I ended up wearing not just any dress but a strapless black dress and heels — not exactly my signature look. But some-times you have to pick your battles. So, in this get-up, I made my wobbly way from table to table after the ceremony in my uncomfortable shoes. I was fulfilling my maid-of-honor duties, greeting and catching up with people as confidently as I could.

I finally landed at a table of my parents' friends. These were folks I had known since I was a child. They had watched me play softball. They had witnessed my home runs and my strikeouts. They had attended my gradua-tion party.

We exchanged pleasantries and then there was an awkward silence. As I was about to thank them for coming and walk away, one woman stood up to get my attention.

"Ash!" she stammered. "We were talking about it, and we want you to know. It is very important that you know… that we love… Nathan Lane!"

The situation was instantly a whole lot more awkward. Why did she feel compelled to mention this well-known gay actor? Did she think it would make me feel better about myself if she said, *Hey, we know about gay people?* Instead, what she highlighted was our differences. Our years of shared history seemed to vanish.

I wanted to say, "Hey, I'm the same old Ash!" but I also started to feel defensive. I broke out in a nervous sweat.

Before I could excuse myself, another woman at the table stood up too. "Ash, have you ever been to San Francisco?"

Yes, I told her, I had friends there.

"Well, we have never been there but we heard it's *fabulous*!" She all but showed me a limp wrist — the gesture that straight people sometimes use to refer to gay people.

Then the next woman stood up and said, "Do you know my hairdresser, Antonio?"

"I'm not sure," I said, politely ignoring her stereotyping of an entire group of people. "But that name sounds familiar…" Like so many of us in the position of the "token" representative, somehow I still wanted to put her at ease.

Their attempt at respect was missing the mark. My mind was racing. Was I the first real live gay person they'd ever met? Did they have no references beyond stereotypes they saw on TV? Did they think all gay people knew each other? And who the hell was Antonio?

By this time, I desperately wanted to get out of there. But in heels, I was not quick on my feet. One last woman stood up. Her brow was furrowed. She was clearly stumped. Everything good had been taken: Hollywood was taken, San Francisco was taken, hairdressers were taken. How was she going to relate her "approval" and support of my lesbianism? All her friends at the table had found some point of connection. She was not about to be shown up by the other women at Table 24.

Suddenly, her frown turned to a smile, "Well, sometimes my husband Tom, here, he wears pink shirts."

Tom's eyes popped. "Well, it was just one time! It was a Susan G. Komen golf benefit, you know, for breast cancer research." He was turning pink himself. "But pink is okay. I mean, anyone can wear pink. Just not me. Except that one time."

I barely managed to say *thanks for coming* before I turned my back and hobbled away. Someone had to stop the carnage. I went back across the ballroom, heading straight to my table. I just *had* to tell my friends all about these absurd comments. It was as if those women thought by sharing their top gay stereotypes with me, they would clearly convey the message: *We know you are gay and we're good with it.* I wanted to laugh to make myself feel better because, in truth, their stereotypes hurt me. I wasn't just "a gay." I was Ash, just as they'd always known me. I knew my frustration would be understood in my own circle.

But a few things happened before I reached my table. I saw my sister with her new husband. They both looked happier than I had ever seen them. I saw relatives who hadn't spoken in a decade having a beer together. I started seeing all the love and connection in the room, and suddenly, the shortcomings of my parents' friends felt a lot less significant. Some of the guests who had never met each other were genuinely connecting. Whether they had known the bride and groom for 20 minutes or 20 years, love and support were bringing people together.

I hadn't yet reached my table when I was stopped by the woman who had brought up Nathan Lane. I was still feeling defensive, but she and her husband seemed to really want to say something. This time the husband spoke. "Ash, we know you can't do this yet, but if you ever have a celebration, we really want to be there to support you." At that time, same-sex marriage was still illegal.

In the time it had taken me to walk away, they'd realized that they had not yet made a real connection with me. Maybe the overwhelming awkwardness of our previous conversation or my lack of a direct reply had motivated them to search me out. Whatever the reason, they made it a point to find me. They weren't going to let our recent interaction be our last. That's what really counted.

Regardless of their political affiliation, these people had always treated my sister and me the same. They loved my parents, who had been high-school sweethearts, and they loved Mandy and me. Now, during this huge celebration, they suddenly realized that I could not legally marry.

They could not reconcile that the law treated Mandy and me differently. I could feel their empathy.

That day, I learned that the door to empathy swings both ways. It suddenly seemed a lot less important to rush back to my circle of friends to make fun of the unworldliness of Table 24 and their Hollywood/San Francisco/hairdresser comments. A light had flipped on in my head: empathy begets more empathy. Sure, I could have gossiped about what these friends of my parents had said. I could have laughed at their inability to jump through the politically correct hoops I had brought with me. I had been in this kind of situation many times before. My first response was always defensive and protective. I would always try to deflect the stereotypes: *Gay people also live outside San Francisco! Not all hairdressers are gay! Get to know real people!*

My usual reaction came from wanting to be seen as the unique individual I was. I was comprised of thousands of traits, only one of them being that I was gay. It is incredibly isolating to be seen only as your differences, as the things that separate you from others. It made me fierce and vigilant, and more times than not, it made me slam the door on understanding where anyone else was coming from. If others couldn't have any empathy for me, why should I have any for them?

But this moment at my sister's wedding was different from many others before it. The Nathan Lane couple showed empathy first. Their efforts instantly made me less rigid and made me feel less isolated. I softened as a result. In their own way, they were stepping up.

If that was the change empathy could make, I thought, what would have happened if I'd extended that empathy to the rest of Table 24? What if I saw their comments from *their* perspective rather than from mine? Instead of being hurt and offended, what if I saw that offering these comments might have been the hardest thing those people had ever done?

On that day, in that space, they were not going to be wildly comfortable treating me as the same old Ash they'd always known. Which was pretty understandable, because I wasn't. I wanted it to be no big deal; it wasn't a big deal to me. But it was to them. *Not necessarily good or bad, just big.*

That is where empathy comes in. In the simplest terms, the other realistic outcome was that they could have said nothing. We'd finish our superficial conversation, and I'd walk away angry that they hadn't made any kind of gesture at all after not seeing me for such a long time. If I was willing to have just an ounce of empathy, it was easy to see that what they were saying was exactly what I wanted to hear, it was just in their own words. Did that make it any less of an effort because they didn't use the terminology I wanted?

When I slowed down, I could see that, actually, they were really trying to build a bridge to me. What more can we ask people to do but try? Just because someone doesn't know our personal experience in-depth does not disqualify them from wanting to show support, wanting to let us know that they care. It takes courage to expand our comfort zones and this should always be encouraged. People hold back and say nothing because they are afraid of saying the wrong thing. But the only thing worse than saying the wrong thing is saying nothing.

Today, if I faced a Table 24, I would stay. I would talk more. I would expand my own comfort zone, and maybe—just maybe—my showing empathy would soften the edges of the interaction enough that we could all feel safe to be ourselves.

Empathy allows us to understand the perspectives and experiences of other people and meet them where they are. It cuts both ways. If we expect empathy, we must be willing to give it, especially with people we see as different. As leaders, often we must give it first. It is our responsibility to practice empathy with ourselves and others while also recognizing when empathy is extended to us. By doing this, we get a much more comprehensive view of the world. It empowers us to make more informed decisions and to take more mindful action.

« Takeaways »

- **Listen without judgment.** The best way to learn about someone's perspective and experience is to simply listen. In order to meet someone where they are, we must completely put aside our agendas. By suspending our own perspective momentarily, we leave behind the preconceptions and judgments that cloud our ability to enter into another's experience. The question is no longer, "Do I agree with this person or not?" but "What makes this person tick?"

- **Avoid writing people off.** This comes on the tail of withholding judgment. One misstatement or stumble or difference of opinion does not make someone our mortal enemy. We are all constantly evolving. When we write people off, we assume they cannot change or that they must change completely before we will accept them. Who wants to interact with that?

- **Show empathy first.** Once we are consistently practicing empathy, we acknowledge that everyone's experience is unique. The Nathan Lane couple clearly showed empathy and courage. They were brave enough to make the effort to find me and continue the conversation. This allowed me to relax and see the interaction with Table 24 in a more empathetic light too. Empathy begets more empathy, and it can take courage to make that first gesture. We don't need to be perfect. We need to be real and relatable.

- **Expand your comfort zone.** When we begin to consciously become more empathetic, we can find ourselves in uncomfortable situations. We hear stories and learn things we have never thought of before or imagine experiences we have never had. We will be put in awkward situations that our past selves would have fled from. But when we step up, we can start to stay longer and listen more openly.

STEP UP

Empathy Challenge:
Have a Genuinely Curious Conversation

Find someone who has a different viewpoint from you (politically or otherwise). Have a conversation with them — not with the intent of changing their mind or judging them, but with the goal of getting to their *why*, with the sole purpose of understanding that person better. That is the heart of true empathy: that we put in the effort to truly understand someone else's experience, feelings, and perspective. Period. No ulterior motive. No personal gain or need to agree. Just to learn what it is like to be someone else.

≫

PILLAR 2

RESPONSIBILITY

Informing Ourselves and Others

We are inherently curious, social creatures. We like to relate to other people. So it's natural that once we feel a connection to those around us, we want to do right by them — or at least respect them. Responsibility is the awareness that our actions have an impact, even if we never hear about it. Therefore, we must act with intention and purpose; this is the logical next step after cultivating empathy. We feel a responsibility to learn more about what it is like to walk in someone else's shoes, and we also want to let others know, with kindness and compassion, when what they are saying and doing is hurtful, even if that's not their intention.

After my first talk went viral, I was working one of my many "real" jobs doing security for a large trade-show company. Within a week, I'd gone from Judy Average to being a minor celebrity. Random strangers were stopping me on the street wherever I went. I was accustomed to people staring at me, especially when I had a shaved head. But now the stares were more inquisitive than judgmental. Suddenly, they were not rooted in fear or misunderstanding but rather in curiosity. They seemed to say, *Wait—how do I know that person?* It was awesome.

In the talk I'd done at Ignite Boulder, I had come out to half a million people explaining that we needed to examine the pejorative use of the word "gay" in our everyday lives. Folks would come up to me and say they never knew that the G-word had such a negative effect. I don't know how many times I heard, "Wait, you just came up on my Facebook feed!" It was so incredibly empowering that it made me want to speak up on behalf of the LGBTQ experience more loudly and more often. It was also something new in my world. I wasn't used to it.

At the trade show, as I was waiting to open the doors an eager crowd was gathering. A woman approached me. "I really liked your Ignite video on YouTube," she said, thanking me for my message.

Overhearing her comment, someone nearby got curious. "Oh, yeah? What was your video about?" he asked. I had gotten used to the compliments, but I'd never had to have an in-person conversation about the substance of the video.

I froze. The name of the talk is "Eliminating 'Gay' as a Pejorative from Our Lexicon," and the first line is, "Hi,

I'm Ash, and I'm SO GAY!" In the video, it's a funny and catchy opening, but I had never outed myself on demand like this before. The potential interaction with this total stranger scared me. What if this guy hated gay people? When someone watches one of my videos, I'm not usually in the room. So when I declare something as personal as my sexuality, I never know if they are offended, enraged, or disgusted. I'm protected. Face to face, in person, I had no protection and no anonymity. A split second was all I had.

I did an instant assessment of this guy. He was white, straight, cis-gendered (meaning not transgendered), heterosexual, and able-bodied. I made the assumption that this guy would never watch a video on coming out as gay. But in my rapid-fire thoughts, I believed he could still get something out of the video. So if I tricked him into watching it, maybe I could accidentally enlighten him.

"It is about word choice, and how the words we use affect other people," I said, which was true —but, come on! Can you think of a more boring YouTube video to watch? If my only goal was to trick this guy into watching it, I should have just said that it was about me and my dog twerking or something. Sure, I was not lying to him, but I was definitely hiding the full set of facts to protect myself from his possible judgment and disdain—and possibly worse. My anticipation and fear of a public altercation were strong enough that I took the easy way out.

The effect of my obscure answer was immediate. The guy nodded politely and looked away. He was not drawn in. In fact, he seemed turned off. It was now unlikely that he would watch the video, and that was a bummer. Worse, I'd sold the guy short. He could have been gay, he could have had a gay kid, or he could have just been a great ally. But I was so worried about him judging me that I made sure I judged him first. In retrospect, my hypocrisy is embarrassing. And that wasn't even the worst part.

When I looked over to the woman who had originally given me the compliment, I saw her smile fade away, her eyes drop, and her shoulders slump. She was visibly disappointed by my response. My heart sank. Even worse than seeing her disappointment was realizing that I had disappointed myself.

Seeing and feeling the disappointment made me realize that if I was going to do this work—if I was going to truly be an active advocate—then I had a responsibility to live my day-to-day life the same way as I appeared on the video. I had to seize the opportunity to be brave, vulnerable, and forthright with my knowledge and position. What I represented to that woman who had complimented me was an honest, out, confident activist who used humor to make an awkward situation relatable and less intense. If I believed the video made people's lives better (which I did), it was my responsibility to step up in everyday situations the same way I advocated online. Taking a stand in a video was easy; living it was harder.

How we operate in the world directly affects others. We may think we exist in a vacuum, and only think about how our actions affect *us*. We might think, *I'm just an ordinary person. How much influence do I really have?* But the truth is we never know when our comments and actions might also influence someone else, including a stranger who may never have the chance to tell us. So it's important for our actions to be in line with who we are — with our most authentic selves.

In truth, as I stepped into this new role of advocate, I faced a lot of new challenges. For example, it was very easy to speak to LGBTQ groups. I had instant credibility. The stories I told — my stories — were often just like other people's: being mistaken for the wrong gender, constantly monitoring situations to make sure I was safe, being careful about where and how I expressed affection with my partner. These were common experiences for the gay community. If what I talked about hadn't happened to other people directly, it had happened to people they knew. They could relate.

But as I started to speak on college campuses, I faced a new challenge. Diversity initiatives went well beyond the LGBTQ community or any single marginalized group. Schools that were taking inclusion seriously expected speakers like me to be able to address diversity from all angles — race, ethnicity, LGBTQ, ability, etc. I started to feel like I wasn't cut out for that. I mean, sure, I could speak for hours about the challenges facing LGBTQ folks, but I have never been followed by a security guard in the store because of the color of my skin. That is not my world or my life experience. Who the hell did I think I was to speak about it?

This came into sharp relief when I was invited to address a liberal arts college in upstate New York as a part of a Martin Luther King Day celebration. The director of the event let me know that some members of the faculty were disappointed to have a white keynote speaker for MLK Day. "I just want you to know what you are walking into," he said. My ultimate fear had come true: that voice in my head that was constantly saying, *Who the hell do you think you are?* was no longer just the voice of self-doubt. Other people actually thought that, too. And I was about to stand on a stage in front of them.

I took a walk to gather myself. I called my sister to ask for some advice. She instantly quoted Dr. King: "'I have a dream that my four little children will one day live in a nation where they will not be judged by the color of their skin but by the content of their character.' It goes both ways, Ash. You've got to step up." I spent my speaking career preaching that people had to be strong enough to be vulnerable. They had to be willing to put themselves out there without embarrassment or shame in order to learn something they didn't know before. Now the shoe was on the other foot. When it came to being gay, I was an expert. When it came to race, I was white and not fully comfortable acknowledging my privilege. I was a rookie. For years I had downplayed the fear of being vulnerable when other people struggled with it around difficult LGBTQ issues. Now that fear was coursing through my veins, and it was more intense than I anticipated. Still, it was time for me to walk my talk.

With every ounce of courage I could muster, I went on stage and attempted to display the content of my character. I tried to be honest, inclusive, fallible, open. I told my stories, but then I asked people of color in the audience for their stories. I invited them to tell me things I would never believe, things I would not know because I walked around in a white skin. They told me about watching white women with their children cross the street to avoid walking by someone black. Or about young black men having to get "the talk" about how to act if they got pulled over by police, which was often a racially charged situation. Many members of the audience nodded in agreement. It seemed that some version of these stories had happened to nearly every person of color in the room.

Then a student brought up a common incident that happened every Halloween. There would be a party, often at a fraternity, and many of the white partygoers would dress up as black celebrities. Blackface was part of the costume. This was accepted by the majority of the white student body and by the university administration. It happened year after year. But it hurt and angered black students. Their frustration with the ignorance of white students and teachers lasted well beyond Halloween.

Let's pause right there for a moment. First, the word "ignorance" has a negative connotation, but here I simply mean a lack of knowledge. There is nothing wrong with ignorance in this sense. It is completely understandable that we do not know what it is like to live with a different color skin or gender or different physical abilities or any of the myriad of differences that exist among humans. So there's no need to feel bad about what we don't know. The point is to educate ourselves, to take an active role in correcting our blind spots.

Black students' frustrations and experiences were foreign to me, but it was transformational to hear about them. I could feel the emotion in the room. Empathetically, I was all in. But I did not fully understand *why* they were frustrated. I had some homework to do.

On the flight home, a million thoughts and questions raced through my mind. I realized that if I wanted to truly be an advocate, if I wanted to have credibility in groups I did not belong to, it was my responsibility to leave my ego at the door and learn from those willing to share their stories with me. When we learn the unique perspectives and histories of those who are different from us, we are empowered with knowledge we didn't have before. That changes the way we see the world, even though we have not lived those lives. I decided to educate myself so that I could come to the next interaction with students with deeper knowledge. I wanted to learn more.

When I got home, I dug around online. I learned that the use of blackface began in the early 1800s in minstrel shows, in which white actors would portray black people in gross caricatures as lazy, stupid, animalistic, and so on. As part of their costume, the actors would darken their skin with polish and burnt cork. These shows were entertainment for white audiences in a culture that regularly dehumanized nonwhite people and that had benefitted greatly from slavery, the ultimate dehumanization.

It's not like blackface or its equivalents are a thing of the distant past. Blackface as "entertainment" existed well into the twentieth century. When Al Jolson, a singer, actor, and comedian in the 1920s, was the most popular entertainer in the United States, he performed exclusively in blackface. These racist portrayals affected people outside of the African American community, too. Native Americans were portrayed as savage Indians by white actors in redface. Mickey Rooney in *Breakfast at Tiffany's* played Mr. Yunioshi, a Japanese neighbor, and wore yellowface, buck teeth, taped eyelids, and nearly every Asian racial stereotypical characteristic. This happened in the context of the anti-Japanese sentiment after World War II. In the 1960s, this kind of blatant racism was palatable to the majority of white Americans.

Many white people today may not find blackface offensive. They may not even know where it comes from. They have black friends, and they just want to be Beyoncé and Jay-Z for Halloween. But context matters. Centuries of these dehumanizing stereotypes help to keep a xenophobic culture and institutionalized racism alive. Blackface is more than someone at a Halloween party painting their face black and putting on an Afro. It has deep roots in a painful past and social problems that still exist today.

Now, most of us strive not to be jerks. We know our actions impact others, and we don't want to unknowingly offend anyone. If we had the essential information—if we had the backstory—we would act differently. But we simply can't change what we are unaware of. When we just can't seem to recognize our blind spots, it might take a well-placed comment from someone else to illuminate our ignorance. We need to be open to that, too.

The flip side to becoming more aware is that eventually we find ourselves in the position to point things out to others. This is a second aspect of responsibility.

The way I see it, my friends and family would *want* to know the backstory. They'd want to make more aware decisions if they could. This perspective gives me confidence to help them avoid being unintentionally offensive. When I come from a place of confidence, I don't come across as aggressive or micromanaging. I'm not conveying my ideas from a place of fear. If I had spoken from a place of confidence to the guy who asked what my video was about, I would have answered in a straightforward way, regardless of what I feared his response would be.

That said, pointing out to people that their words or behaviors are hurting someone else is not always easy or comfortable. I get it. No one wants to be the bad guy, and no one wants a lecture. But clueing someone in can be as awkward or as straightforward as telling someone they have spinach in their teeth. You know the spinach is there because you can see it. But they can't. Do you tell them or not? You don't want to embarrass them. And yet they would likely be much more embarrassed if they knew how long that chunk of green has been there. You clue them in as a favor, to save them further embarrassment. It's the same with any kind of ignorance. If you did not know the history of blackface and were considering wearing blackface as part of a costume, you might appreciate a friend calmly and compassionately educating you on its history before you make a fool of yourself or, worse, offend an entire section of society.

When I tap into my genuine desire to help others, I can point things out without judging or criticizing. This is how cultural change begins and is sustained. It doesn't come from top-down dictates from legislators or administrators but rather from grassroots conversations between individuals. When we can have conversations with each other about the things that really matter, then all of us have a chance of speaking and acting with true respect.

As leaders, we don't want someone to change their offensive behaviors because we tell them so. Then they just mute that behavior around us, which is not sustainable and misses the point. Change means people understand the impact of their behavior on others, and they *want* to make adjustments. They want their behavior to align with their values. It is not about being politically correct but about not wanting their actions to be hurtful.

This hit home for me in November 2018 when I was having a conversation with the brilliant Amber Hikes, who was at the time the executive director of the Philadelphia Mayor's Office of LGBTQ Affairs. Amber and I had recently spoken at an event together, and I was fascinated by her talk on intersectional allyship, which means standing up for and advocating on behalf of a marginalized group that we are not part of. During our conversation, Amber shared with me her understanding of the difference between calling someone *in* and calling someone *out*—key tools in embracing responsibility. Calling someone *in* means pulling friends aside to let them know, gently, that something they did or said was offensive. We know that if they had the same information we have, they would want to make some changes. We do not view our friends' ignorance as a fault but rather as an opportunity. Just like pointing out the spinach in their teeth.

Calling *out*, on the other hand, means taking an immediate, definitive action to stop egregious behavior. This is more about setting boundaries than pulling someone aside for a conversation. If a new member joins my soccer team and uses an offensive slur in reference to the other team, it would be appropriate to call her out on the spot, to nip it in the bud. Both approaches are necessary tools. An effective leader knows when to use which one.

Amber gave me an example of calling in that really stuck with me. At a meeting of the Philadelphia city marketing department, the staff was checking language on a brochure. They wanted to make sure that the text was correct and up to their standards. This was a socially sensitive group of people who were creating documents on inclusivity. Their intentions could not have been any purer. But in going through the text, someone objected to using the word "handicapped."

"This is approved language," said the project leader. "It is how we refer to people with disabilities in all of our communications."

The person who objected to this word asked if anyone knew where it derived from. No one did.

"It comes from 'cap in hand,' which refers to a time when the only means of survival for people with disabilities was to beg on the street, asking for money by holding out their caps."

When Amber told me this story, I blurted out, "Wow! I had no idea!"

"That is what the entire room said," she told me. "'We had no idea.'" Instantly, the word was no longer an acceptable characterization of a whole group of people. It wasn't the meaning they or the city wanted to convey.

"No one knew," Amber said. "But once we know, we can never forget."

That one person who spoke up could have remained silent. Who wants to sound like the politically correct police? But she overcame her hesitation to act: her desire to share what she knew outweighed her fears of any social or professional repercussions. She called everyone at that meeting *in* by letting them know the history and context of the word. Knowing the facts allowed the team to come to terms with their ignorance. There was no shaming. It was just the facts, which eliminated any reflex to respond with emotion or resistance.

When our inner sense of responsibility is aligned with our outer actions, we know that the greater good of the community takes priority over our own reluctance to speak in a straightforward way, to be informed, or to act. It is not about us individually but about the impact we can have on the broader society by acting with purpose because our sense of responsibility drives us to do so.

« Takeaways »

- **Lead by example.** We cannot always control situations, but we can always control how we act. To lead by example is powerful. Imagine if you found yourself in the middle of a conflict and your kids were watching. Or your mom. Or your best friend. What would you want them to learn? How would you want them to see you? You may never know how you affect people, but you always have the opportunity to lead in the way you show up.

- **Choose openness and vulnerability.** No one wants to appear ill-informed or ignorant. We don't want to look stupid or unenlightened. But when we avoid admitting our shortcomings or lack of knowledge, we prevent ourselves from growing. Similarly, when we take responsibility for learning what it is like to be someone other than us, we must be open to whatever that looks like. We have to be willing to examine the parts of ourselves that we are not necessarily proud of. That effort is counter to our instinct for self-preservation, so we must intentionally choose to be open and vulnerable in order to allow learning and growing to happen.

- **Do the homework.** By the same token, it is not solely the responsibility of other people to educate us on their experiences. Part of responsibility is doing the work to learn what it is like to walk in someone else's shoes. Whether we study academic papers or watch YouTube videos, broadening our understanding of other human experiences is key to stepping up.

■ **Clue people in.** Once we become better informed, we have a responsibility to share our knowledge. Remember the spinach-in-the-teeth thing? Clueing people in does not mean getting up on a soapbox to give a condescending lecture. It means being aware of the fact that there are people who are exactly where we were before we knew better. How would we have liked that knowledge to have been passed on to us? Through kind and compassionate conversations, we can become a resource for others, to help them avoid or correct missteps.

STEP UP
Responsibility Challenge:
Explore an Unfamiliar Issue

In our current political climate, we are bombarded with news of controversial issues every day: immigration, racism, gentrification, political polarization, a myriad of local debates. Maybe there's one in your community right now.

For this challenge, pick a topic that is close to home but that you don't know much about. If you can't articulate the different sides of the debate, then chances are you don't quite understand what the issue is or what's at stake.

Once you have your topic, dig a little deeper.

Part of responsibility is empathy, or taking the time to understand both sides of the discussion. We don't need to agree with either one, but we can at least know where each side is coming from. This empowers us to think for ourselves about the issue.

There's no need to write a dissertation on the subject. Just empower yourself with a little more knowledge than you had before. What's one more thing you know about the topic now? By educating ourselves, we are better equipped to engage in *civil* discourse.

≋

PILLAR 3

COURAGE

Acting Despite the Fear

I t takes guts to be the person brave enough to do the harder right thing instead of the easier wrong thing. In the same way, standing up to the bully on the playground is an act of courage. Making an unpopular decision of integrity at work instead of taking the low road takes courage, too. Where does that courage come from? Why do some folks have it while other folks don't? We usually frame courage as a trait similar to being outgoing or having a great sense of humor. It can seem like something we just come into this world with. But what if courage was not an inborn quality but rather a skill? What if it was something rooted in all of us that could be developed? If that were the case, then everyone has courage, and it's just waiting to show itself. It can be practiced and trained the same way we strengthen a muscle. So how do we discover that muscle and start flexing it?

Ideally, we would train our courage muscles logically and progressively, identifying low-stakes opportunities to practice. But life can be unpredictable. Plus, what seems like low stakes to you might feel like incredibly high stakes to me.

Even though what we fear is personal, that fear response is universal. It is actually hardwired into our nervous systems. When we encounter a threat, real or perceived, it sets off a chemical reaction in our bodies that dictates how we respond. The first reaction is the release of stress hormones such as cortisol and adrenaline, commonly described as fight, flight, or freeze hormones. Imagine waking up in the middle of the night to see something that looks like a person in the hallway. Our breath quickens and our fists clench. We get a queasy feeling in the pit of our stomach. Our instinct is to either try to combat this threat, run from it, or hold still, hoping it will go away. It is a very animalistic response.

When we turn on the light and see that the form that looked like a person is just a coat rack, those hormones are already streaming through our body. They can't immediately turn off. Stress hormones do not care if the threat is real or not. They don't worry about the details. To them, a threat is a threat is a threat. This explains why we have trouble falling back to sleep right away after we realize our mistake. We're too jacked up.

Since these hormones are a biological occurrence, we will never eliminate them. We wouldn't want to since they are designed to keep us safe and alive. The challenge is how to deal with them when they come up in situations that, ultimately, are not life-threatening. As with anything, practice helps. When we push our individual comfort zones, we see whether we can overcome the natural set point for our fears.

Erik Weihenmayer is an adventurer who has made pushing boundaries his life's work. At the age of fourteen he began to pursue rock climbing. At the same time, he also began losing his vision to retinoschisis, an eye disease. As the disease progressed, not only did he keep climbing, but he became a professional athlete. In 2001, he summited Mount Everest, becoming the first blind person ever to do this. By 2008, he had completed the Seven Summits, ascending the highest points on every continent. He is only one of 150 mountaineers to have done so.

But Erik wasn't done. In his quest to keep pushing himself, he kayaked the entire 277 miles of the Colorado River through the Grand Canyon, some of the most treacherous whitewater in the world. As for many of us, one accomplishment led to another challenge. When he became comfortable with a certain level of fear, he ratcheted up the fear level for the next challenge. His previous fear "ceiling" became his new "floor." He is a great example of someone who is constantly practicing courage.

Many of us cannot imagine overcoming fear the way Erik did, let alone attempting the adventures he does, even with all of our senses intact. Erik is an exceptional human.

But we don't need to worry about matching other people's achievements. We just need to be sure we are pushing our own boundaries. For us, a more realistic challenge—one that still stretches us—might be to train for and run a 5K race. When we've done that, we might then decide our next goal will be a 10K.

People all around us are courageous every day, in ways that don't make front page news. Often, the situations are personal and therefore hidden from public view. Such situations range from having the courage to date again after heartbreak to walking into a new classroom for the first time to saying something out loud that we've been thinking or going somewhere where we've been very uncomfortable in the past.

For the longest time, the scariest place for me was a public bathroom.

As I've said, I am gender nonconforming. That means I'm biologically female and I identify as a woman, but my gender expression does not fit with what people usually think of as female. My hair is short. I don't wear makeup. My jawline is strong. I feel most comfortable in men's jeans and button-downs. I do not deny that, to a passing glance, I could be mistaken for a man. That gender expression is a part of who I am and it is how I feel most comfortable.

So when I walk into a public bathroom, more times than not, one of three things happens. Little kids point and giggle. Or adults do a double take and stare. Or third and worst of all, someone confronts me. "This is the women's restroom. You don't belong here!"

This has happened to me for years. The first few times I was startled and then offended. In the moment, I did not have the luxury of being scared or feeling hurt. I was in full fight, flight, or freeze mode. My nervous system perceived life-threatening danger and amped up the stress hormones to meet it. I saw my options as freezing in place, running away, or getting ready for battle. My emotions came later when the confrontation was over. I'd be overwhelmed with self-doubt: *Should I just appear more feminine to make everyone feel better? Was there something really wrong with me? Did I have a right to feel safe?*

This happened over and over and over again until just thinking about going into a women's restroom got my stress hormones flowing. I started to expect trouble. I refused to fight back and become confrontational in return, even though I felt attacked. I never had the courage to actually say something. The risk was just too great. Would I trip over my words? Would I burst into tears? Whose side would the bystanders choose? Instead, I would just try to disappear, to get through the whole process as quickly and invisibly as possible. My expectation was to feel embarrassed and humiliated. Anything short of that was a success.

I travel about half the year to give talks and attend other work events, so I spend an unfortunate amount of time in public bathrooms. Daily bathroom stress was a way of life for me.

When we feel disrespected by others, the pain runs deep. When our experiences or identities are dismissed or minimized, it can feel dehumanizing. We can feel categorized or boxed in by other people's biases, assumptions, and fears. Here is what it feels like to me: when I am confronted in a public bathroom, I am instantly flooded with emotion. I want to scream at the top of my lungs and at the same time crawl in a hole and hide. I feel like there is a spotlight on me, yet at the same time I feel invisible. We have all felt these conflicting emotions in whatever places or situations are the most challenging for us. At work, at home, with our bodies — in public bathrooms — whatever it is. Who hasn't felt furiously mad and overwhelmingly sad at the same time?

In moments of defiance, I would fantasize about making a witty retort to anyone who questioned my presence in the bathroom. I'd deliver some perfectly crafted yet seemingly off-the-cuff response. That'd show them. I'd stand up for all the times I'd slunk away dejectedly. But most of the time, I didn't say anything at all. I'd just internalize the comments and continue to lower my expectations for humanity. It seemed like the more I expected conflict, the more conflict I got. To alter my experiences in public bathrooms, I needed to find the courage to change how I responded, not just accept how things were or to feel that I was somehow wrong for being me.

It happened one day about a decade ago in the Chicago O'Hare Airport.

For me, all public bathrooms are bad, but airport bathrooms are the worst. Airports are not the most relaxing places anyway. People are rushing and stressed, worried about making their flights, about passing through security and staying safe. The stress is contagious and the rules seem endless: *Do not leave your bags unattended. Finish your liquids. Take off your shoes and belt.* Most of us are not super-paranoid, but at the airport we become hypervigilant and maybe a bit irrational. See something; say something! If we see something suspicious we need to report it immediately. The idea that the most basic items—plastic bottles and shoes—could be vehicles for destruction is enough to send our stress hormones into overdrive.

During this frantic, high-adrenalin rush, we can sometimes also stop noticing the people around us. Why should we engage with those we will never see again, who have nothing to do with us, and who, frankly, are just taking way too long to get through security?

Instead, when our stress hormones are going full tilt, we lose the ability to slow down and assess. We don't give the rational part of our brain the time it needs to catch up. I know that my appearance is challenging to some folks. When people encounter me walking down the street or hanging out at a restaurant, they usually have the time and space to "figure me out" and get comfortable with my difference. But in the hyperstressed environment of airports, that time and space are nonexistent. People become like parents at Little League games: in their normal lives, they are rational, contributing humans. But on the field, they will go to blows over their eight-year-olds' strike zones.

Since stress levels are already high at airports, the bathrooms become extra challenging for me. The problem is not people's quizzical stares and double takes. I am accustomed to that. What gets me is the aggression. It's the presumption that I am a predator. It's like I'm the same as an unmarked bag sitting on its own waiting to explode when all I am actually doing is try to pee just like everyone else.

Going through the O'Hare Airport that holiday season, I sensed that the already gonzo energy in the airport was now on steroids. There was double the number of folks travelling, and all of them were loaded with stuff—coats, hats, gifts, additional luggage, and additional people, who they may or may not have been getting along with. You could almost smell the stress in the air.

But Mother Nature didn't care; I had to pee. I navigated my way through the crowds to the bathroom, rolling my little suitcase behind me. My survival mode kicked in. I entered the bathroom, keeping my head down and avoiding eye contact, as usual. It took 5 seconds for a woman to walk up behind me and grab my shoulder. She was in her fifties, brown curly hair, about my height, with an expression of fear mixed with anger.

"Hey! This is the women's bathroom," she said in a voice loud enough for the entire restroom to hear. "You're in the wrong place. What kind of pervert are you? Do I need to call security?"

All of a sudden, the spotlight was on me. Everyone stared. The tension in the bathroom was palpable. Everyone was on high alert. I was, too. I was being physically restrained and threatened. I was being accused of a serious violation—of being a pervert. My brain perceived an imminent threat and went into fight-flight-freeze mode. My body stiffened. My heart rate shot up. My hands were sweating and clenched.

Unfortunately for this woman, the debt I felt society owed me from years of this kind of confrontation was coming due on her shift. I didn't cower this time as I had countless times in the past. Instead, I spun around and faced her head on. My shoulders were not slumped as usual. I didn't drop my gaze to avoid eye contact. I met her gaze with a fierce one of my own. That alone shocked her. But I wasn't done. Because it was *that time of the month* for me, I pulled a tampon out of my pocket and—inspired by one of my favorite poems, called "SwingSet," by the amazing slam poet Andrea Gibson—I unleashed the fury I'd bottled up for decades.

"Your timing is perfect. I was just about to go in this stall and put in this tampon. So if you want to come with me and see if I am indeed in the right place, that would be great."

Her eyes were wide open, her mouth agape. She looked like I had just slapped her. Everything in the bathroom stopped. People stopped washing and drying their hands. Even the water coming out of the automatic faucets stopped.

Everyone who had been staring continued to stare, but not how they always had. Now they had a new curiosity. Maybe not respect, but they were definitely intrigued. What would happen next? The woman took a few steps back. She muttered something under her breath and dropped her gaze.

Truth be told, I was as shocked by what I had said as she was. But I was also emboldened by this swell of courage.

Seeing that I had the floor, I took one more shot. I walked toward the stall.

"You sure? No? All right, I guess you'll never know then." I entered the stall and shut the door. For the first time in decades, I was actually smiling in a public bathroom. I felt more like myself than I had for a long time.

To this day, I don't know where my courage came from to act differently. Perhaps I was fed up with years of saying nothing. Or perhaps my frustration with this never-ending situation overcame my fear of the consequences. Or maybe on some level I realized that the situation was not going to change unless I was the one to make the change.

For a while after that incident, I carried a tampon in my pocket everywhere I went. I would walk out of the house and touch every pocket, taking inventory: keys, wallet, phone, tampon. Check! This still didn't eliminate my anxiety when I walked into a public bathroom, but I had changed the narrative that had run in my head for a very long time. Instead of accepting my "place" as outcast, I resolved that if conflict came up, I would meet it head-on instead of fleeing and feeling ashamed and angry in private. I was armed and ready. This response was more in line with how I saw myself outside of these confrontations too. I found the courage to be me, to be more authentic, even in situations that challenged me to the core.

Courage is not the absence of fear. It is the ability to face that fear head-on and act *in spite of it*. Without fear, we are naïve at best and negligent at worst. When we are trying to develop bravery, our goal is not to eliminate fear; that's not just unrealistic, it's also unhealthy. Courage means developing the ability to manage that fear and to voluntarily act in opposition of what it evokes.

Think of firefighters whose job is to run into burning buildings. They do not lack fear. In fact, they of all people know what devastation a fire can wreak. Experience has taught them how to be safe despite the risks they're taking. They have years of training that equip their brains to manage stress hormones and not get stuck in fight, flight, or freeze mode like the average person's. So they are better suited to recognize fear and make clear-headed choices in spite of it. This is the root of courage — mastering fear.

The good news is that we *can* change our response to stress. But our fears cannot be jarred out of us, they must be coaxed. Our neuroplasticity — our brain's ability to rewire old patterns and create new pathways — happens slowly. Exposure to fear and uncomfortable situations is the best way to get a handle on our anxieties and phobias. In other words, we put ourselves in these situations over and over until our willingness to act is greater than our fear. This is how we slowly overcome what terrifies us. And this sets us up to engage in courageous acts.

Science backs this up. In 2010, Israeli researchers, headed by Uri Nili from the Weizmann Institute of Science, conducted a study to find the neurological source of "courage." They defined courage as the "performance of voluntary action opposed to that promoted by ongoing fear." Using functional magnetic resonance imaging (fMRI), researchers were able to measure and map their subjects' brain activity during a task that required courage. Half of their subjects were afraid of snakes and the other half were experienced snake handlers. A live, nonpoisonous snake was put on a trolley close to them while they were in the scanner. Subjects had to decide whether to bring the trolley closer to them or send it away. Sure enough, the brain imagery showed that the part of the brain that registers rewards was active when subjects faced their fear and acted courageously. This part of their brains was not active when they succumbed to their fear.

What this means is that if we are afraid of snakes, repeated exposure to them in low-risk situations lowers our fear response. In other words, we are rewarded for our courage by having less fear. That does not mean we should go out and buy a pet anaconda tomorrow and live with it slithering around our homes. But when we get that fear feeling in the pit of our stomachs, we can notice it and then choose how we want to respond. That in itself is a nontypical response. The next time the same challenging situation happens, we may still be experiencing that familiar sinking feeling, but it will likely be less paralyzing. We can override our primitive need to fight, flee, or freeze.

How do we make that first bold step? How do we coax ourselves to be courageous? First, we can start by taking the simple step of not running away. That in itself is choosing the harder right over the easier "wrong," or over inaction. We can also highlight and acknowledge the small acts of courage, the moments of bravery that are not always on display, but that take no less courage. Think of someone walking into their first day at a new job. Some people are super-social and try to make friends right away. They introduce themselves to everyone in the office and attempt to make connections immediately. Others put their nose down and do their work as an attempt to prove their worth before they try connecting personally. Those tactics and other methods in between are in pursuit of feeling safe. Both require dealing with an uncomfortable situation.

It is our responsibility to see the innate courage in ourselves, to overcome our fears and choose the brave action as much as we can. In time and with practice, we might also become an example for someone else.

We all need heroes to inspire us. Most of the time, courage is an everyday practice that no one else will ever know about. But sometimes it can have a much bigger effect than we intended. Rosa Parks's simple act of not moving to the back of the bus sparked a powerful movement. No doubt there were countless times before the Montgomery Bus Boycott when she had moved to the back of the bus, maybe muttering to herself or her friends, "One of these days, I won't move. Can you imagine if we just didn't move?"

The truth is that Rosa Parks was not the first person to refuse to give up her seat. She was just the one who made the front page and the one who history remembers best. There is no question that she felt fear. So did all the other people who refused to give up their seats before her. They were just as brave. They knew fully the possible repercussions of their defiance. Today Claudette Colvin and Mary Louise Smith are not as well known as Rosa Parks, but their impact was just as great. When we practice courage as everyday leaders, recognition is irrelevant.

On our journey to stepping up, we must be willing to feel the fear and act anyway. This is how true change happens. If we want to change the world around us, first we must have the courage to make the first move.

« Takeaways »

- **Feel the fear.** Pushing fear away might have served a good purpose in the past. But facing our fears ultimately leads to new opportunities — if not right away, then down the road when we're more comfortable with them. Give yourself permission to feel fear. That fear response is natural and it is how we know we are doing something outside of our comfort zone. If we do not feel the fear, we can't practice courage.

- **Reset your boundaries.** Venturing into uncharted territory makes us uncomfortable, but it is also how we grow. So challenge yourself. Once you have overcome that challenge, move your boundaries a bit further. The stronger that courage muscle becomes, the greater the challenge required to keep it growing.

- **Practice courage every day.** We don't train for a 5K race by running only once a month. We start with short runs, and we cross-train on off days. We may run for 1 minute and walk for 2, repeating until we complete 30 minutes. The point is we must start. We slowly and intentionally build up to our challenge by training those muscles every day in different ways. Identify low-stakes situations that make you fearful but that also carry little risk. These are perfect situations to try to overcome fear that is not debilitating, just unpleasant.

STEP UP

Courage Challenge:
Stay in the Uncomfortable

We find ourselves in awkward situations every day. We hear an inappropriate joke, we're asked to do something we don't agree with, or someone reacts to us in an aggressive way. For some of us, the first thing we do is look for the door. It's normal to want to flee what's awkward and find a more comfortable situation in which we can feel more ourselves. It's the same as when we move away from a fire if it is too hot. Our brains send us signals to shift to a more comfortable — or safer — position.

Courage comes when we are willing to act in opposition to the fear. To step up, we must expose ourselves to situations in which we can begin the practice of mastering fear rather than eliminating it as quickly as possible.

Next time you find yourself in an awkward situation, don't run. You don't have to have the greatest interaction of your life, you just need to endure the discomfort. That in itself is an action that opposes fear. You can start small. Maybe you are shy and want to challenge your shyness by chatting with the cashier at the grocery store or with the barista at the coffee shop. Maybe you worry that you will be wasting everyone's time or that you'll get tongue-tied. Maybe you don't want to step out of your comfort zone.

Courage lies in taking a new action, in doing something different. Start by taking one small step. Say hello, talk about the weather. That's it. Simple, nothing big. If the cashier or the barista doesn't return your friendly gesture, it's not the end of the world. Although it might feel awkward, the interaction will be over soon. If the person engages you in some light conversation, however, then your reward is high.

This is just one example. What's yours?

Stay in the uncomfortable just a few moments longer than you usually do and see what happens.

PILLAR 4

GRACE

Keeping Our Eyes on the Prize

When we finally come into our own, we find the courage to be who we truly are. Then we can take the world by storm — or at least our own little corner of the world. But courage without grace can also allow aggression to sneak into our outlook and behavior. If we're not careful, it can turn into self-righteousness. We might find ourselves intentionally seeking out situations in which to practice our "courage." We do our brave deeds without realizing that any collateral damage from those deeds is our responsibility, too. Then we can become the ones causing the trouble. In a lot of cases, we need to pause instead and take a deep breath before we engage. Having grace builds on that pause, helping us to consider our higher purpose and the impact of our actions.

Are we about to do more damage or move the conversation forward?

In the vast majority of uncomfortable situations we experience, our life is not at risk, although we may respond as if it is. Flooded with stress hormones, we kick into that primal fight, flight, or freeze response we talked about in the last chapter. But stress hormones have counterparts known as happy hormones, such as serotonin, that make us social, empathetic, and compassionate. These are the hormones that wrangle the stress hormones and bring us back to reality when what we perceived as an intruder in our homes turns out to be just a coat rack. Our bodies release happy hormones when we hug a friend or finish a race or have a baby. They make us rational. They allow us to take in the bigger picture rather than staying in the narrow scope that fear creates.

Naturally, we want the happy hormones to be more prevalent in our system than stress hormones. We want more serotonin than cortisol. But how do we get there?

I'll give you the bad news first.

Stress hormones have three advantages over happy hormones. First, stress hormones have been around for about 150 million years with the sole purpose of keeping us alive. They have done a really good job. The part of our brain that signals the release of these hormones is very simple and primitive. It is not worried about being politically incorrect. It is just trying to not get eaten by something bigger. Some folks call this the reptilian brain. We are born with this part of ourselves fully developed.

In contrast, happy hormones are released by a part of the brain that develops over time. We *learn* rationality. We are not born with it.

The second advantage stress hormones have is that their signals travel a shorter distance than those of happy hormones. Imagine someone sitting in front of you with a balloon and a pin. You know they are going to pop it. They tell you they are going to pop it. You watch them hold the pin and approach the balloon. The rational part of your brain is fully prepared for the reality that is going to happen. But even so, when the balloon pops, you jump. You can't help it. Within milliseconds, you reason that the loud sound is that of the balloon, but the stress hormones still make you startle. When a threat arises, stress hormones hit the system first.

If we have a vision for long-term change, it is critical that we keep the big picture in our sights while navigating the smaller interactions. For my part, it took courage for me to stand up for myself when I was confronted in the Chicago O'Hare airport bathroom. It took courage to act in opposition to the fear I felt. Because I had avoided facing my fear for so long, I lashed out. But once I chose to stand my ground that first time, reacting that way became my new normal. I began meeting aggression with aggression so that I would never be caught on my heels again. After a while, I realized that any time I even *perceived* a threat—even just someone doing a double take—my fists were up. It didn't matter if someone was actually looking past me to see if their friend had walked into the restaurant yet. I left no potential conflict unengaged.

After some time, I decided I wanted to stop doing the shock-and-awe routine. That no longer felt authentic to me. The pendulum was swinging too far the other way, and I was now *initiating* conflict. I knew my impact on the greater good would be more significant if I was less confrontational and more cooperative. I wanted to balance my courage with grace.

Having grace is not only a higher-level skill. It also allows us to become a resource for people who want to be more inclusive but don't have all the tools yet. We have the courage to act, as well as the grace to explain the *why* of our actions, our outlooks, and our values to the broader community. We confirm that our actions are never solely about *me* but rather always about *we*. My aggressive response to the woman in the bathroom had an effect, and that effect was my responsibility, too. My past hurt and previous interactions were real. But I needed to be conscious of the relationships I wanted to have in the present and in the future. Next time, in some similar situation, that woman might not even say anything to me or someone like me. She might just immediately call the authorities. If I really wanted her to take the time to *see* people, I needed to take the time to help her (and anyone else within earshot) understand what her hostile comment made me feel—embarrassed, unseen, unwelcome. Communicating like this would take more care, more calm, more vulnerability, more engagement. That was an entirely new level of skill. That kind of action required grace.

When we see every experience as an opportunity to do good, to positively impact the world around us, even in the heat of the moment, we practice grace. We take the conversation beyond our immediate circle of peers who already agree with us. We know we are playing the long game. This broader perspective allows us to give our happy hormones time to catch up with the stress hormones in our body. If our instinctual response is fight, flight, or freeze, grace gives us time to allow happy hormones to counter the stress response. As we know, happy hormones help us to act more rationally. What I learned is that courage has consequences. We need to be mindful of those consequences, both the ones that affect us and the ones that affect others.

There was a moment at a job several years ago when I had the perfect opportunity to practice grace. There will always be some kind of conflict in our lives, whether it's someone cutting in front of us, interpersonal disagreements, or something else. We don't have to search out these situations — they find us. In 2011, I was still in my phase of seeking out conflict. My default mode was aggressive. During this time, I was working at a diner in Boulder, Colorado, called the South Side Walnut Cafe. The beauty of the place was its authenticity. From top to bottom, each member of the staff exuded uniqueness. It was the quirkiest, most amazing group of employees I'd ever worked with. It was also why the café had such a strong following. The owners wanted us to be ourselves, and that showed in every decision they made. Wear a tutu to work? Fine. Shave your head? No big deal. Just don't spill the coffee, and make sure the food goes out hot.

For so many of us, it was the first time we'd worked in an environment that not only accepted us but *celebrated* our individuality. Everybody was very much themselves. We had all kinds of tattoos, hair colors, piercings, and clothing styles. We could reinvent ourselves each day if we felt like it. As a staff member or as a customer, we were hard-pressed to find someone we could not relate to. It was a happy place to work, and it was a happy place to eat because people were real. When you have lived mostly on the margins of acceptability, this is huge.

During my time there, I was feeling newly empowered to express myself exactly as I was. After holding myself in for many, many years, I was now letting everything out. I admit that I also went through phases of militant lesbian intensity. This ranged from not shaving my armpits to quoting Ani DiFranco lyrics as gospel.

Depending on the bagginess of my cargo shorts or how recently I had shaved my head, I would often get a certain question. It was usually a little kid who would spring it on me: "Are you a boy or are you a girl?" An awkward silence would come across the kid's table. The dad would nervously shuffle his newspaper like he hadn't heard anything, and the mom would shoot a *what did you just say?* look at her child. I would say nothing, but inside I would be seething. My head would fill with judgmental questions directed at the parents. How dare you come into a place like this and let your kid ask me a question like that? Don't you come here for the diversity? Do you just buy your girls dolls and your boys trucks? Have you never met a lesbian before?

It took months of conversations with coworkers, usually at the end of our shifts as we rolled silverware, to realize that I was getting very worked up about these situations and needed to say something when they came up. Every time I walked up to a table with a kid between the ages of four and ten years old, I was ready to fight. My stress hormones were always flowing! This is a terrible way to go through life. It's also an awful way to try and make a living when you're working for tips, not to mention flat-out frightening for the kids.

So I decided that next time a child asked me this question, I would respond. I knew it would be a hard conversation, but I was ready. Within a matter of weeks, it happened. I walked up to greet my table, and a little girl popped the question: "Are you a boy or are you a girl?" Then followed the familiar awkward silence. Except this time, I was ready. I felt the familiar urge to go all Women's Studies 101 on this table: I had my Gloria Steinem quotes. I had my Betty Friedan quotes. I was going to bust out a little bit from *The Vagina Monologues*. I took a deep breath to assess my opposition. But just as I was about to unload, I realized that staring back at me was a four-year-old girl in a pink dress. I wasn't facing off some macho challenger; my "opponent" was just a kid. Her question was simple and came out of an honest curiosity.

I took another deep breath and squatted down next to her. Instead of my well-planned tirade, I said, "Yeah, I know it's kind of confusing. My hair's short. My clothes are baggy, but I'm a girl. You know how sometimes you like to wear your princess dress and other times you like to wear your comfy jammies? Well, I'm more of a 'comfortable jammies' kind of girl."

The kid looked me dead in the eye, and without missing a beat she said, "My favorite pajamas are purple with pink fish. Can I have a pancake, please?"

And that was it. Her response was not to engage in the feminist duel of the century. It was just, *Oh, all right. You're a girl. How about that pancake?* It was the easiest hard conversation I'd ever had. Sure, I could have dropped my feminist manifesto all over that table. I would have felt better—for a little bit. It would have made up for all the times when I hadn't said anything before. The kid would have missed my meaning completely, and her parents would have felt exponentially more awkward than they already did. Most of all, I would have missed an opportunity to create meaningful change in myself and connect with the people I waited on.

Looking back, I can say unequivocally that instant changed my life. That kid taught me in a moment how disarming it was to be real, to be authentic, and to be honest: *Not every situation was loaded.* Sometimes a question was just a question. That interaction was brief, but I connected with that girl. We *connected.* The simple act of connecting changed a "them" into an "us." I probably was the only gender non-conforming lesbian that girl had ever interacted with, and perhaps her parents also. Now we'd all had a decent experience in spite of the tension. We'd bonded. Change comes from how we use grace to connect with people in our daily lives, even in moments where we feel tense or triggered. Especially in moments that require courage. When we practice grace, we realize that our actions have a higher purpose. We become driven by something bigger than ourselves.

Grace often has a religious connotation, but when I speak about grace in the context of stepping up, I'm talking about the conscious choices we make in how we interact within the world. Are we reactive? Aggressive? Patient? What impact are we having? Is our action in line with our values?

To me, grace means not going with our worst fears or assumptions. It means that we give people the benefit of the doubt. We acknowledge our fear and the response that cortisol creates, but when we think of the higher purpose, we try to cultivate the serotonin instead. Sometimes we have to give a big benefit of the doubt, and there's no question that can be challenging. To lead with grace requires that we are willing to trust and forgive the person or people we are in perceived opposition to. It means keeping our reactivity in check and keeping our highest purpose in sight. Physiologically, our bodies *want* to be calm. We just tend to get triggered by our fear.

An example of grace under pressure is the performance of Jackie Robinson, widely known as the player to break the color barrier in Major League Baseball. What made Robinson great was not that he was named Rookie of the Year in 1947 or that two years later he was named National League MVP or that he played in every all-star game between 1949 and 1954 as well as six World Series. That just makes him a great ballplayer. What makes him an icon is that he accomplished all of that while facing the external pressures and distractions of being the first African American to play in the Majors.

When the Dodgers signed him, their concern was not his baseball skills, since he had clearly displayed those in the Negro League. The question was whether he could handle all of the outcry, taunting, attacks, and isolation that came with being the first black player in the Major Leagues.

When opposing players taunted him, Jackie Robinson knew he could not respond heatedly. It didn't matter if his anger was justified or not. He couldn't lash out for getting pitches thrown at his head or for being refused lodging at the same hotel as his teammates. His role as de facto ambassador for the integration of baseball was unavoidable, so he did not have the luxury of being reactive. By default, Robinson was playing the long game, which had significantly more power than one heated exchange in which he indulged his emotions. After he retired from Major League Baseball, he was able to leverage his celebrity power into a life of activist work.

When Robinson faced discrimination, he did not get to pick his allies. If he waited for every player, coach, and umpire to fully come to terms with their racial biases before he considered them allies, it would have been a lonely season and a lonely life. We do not exist in a vacuum. When we can see others' efforts not only from the perspective of what *we* need but rather the perspective of what others can offer, then we are starting to find empathy, and from that we can find grace.

When our goal is to make change, the distractions are easier to block out. We have all stood on that precipice where we see conflict coming on. Often, all we can think about is how we're going to survive it. Grace means taking a pause to see the situation for exactly what it is: not the amalgamation of all of our previous unpleasant experiences nor what we expect it to be. Rather, a new situation is a unique experience that has never happened before. If every situation is new, then we have the power to decide how to respond. We don't have to repeat our previous reactions. As leaders, we see every new challenge as an opportunity.

Easy to say but harder to do. In the heat of the moment, when our pulse is racing, we might not be thinking rationally. We might forget our best intentions. That's common. Just remember, BOBA: Breathe in, Observe, Breathe out, Act. Deliberate breathing calms the nervous system. It gives us a moment to pause and activates the parasympathetic nervous system, which slows the heart rate and brings equilibrium to the body. The effect is that it calms us from the inside out, allowing us time to remember our bigger purpose.

When our primal instincts take over, our vision becomes myopic. When presented with a conflict, we are pressured both externally and internally to make the quick decision. We lose the big picture, be it a broader scope or long-term perspective, when we are solely using our reptilian brain. Grace is finding the perfect balance of courage and patience. When we practice grace, we are empowered to be brave enough to do the right thing while taking the necessary pause to consider the full impact of our actions on ourselves and our greater community.

« Takeaways »

■ **Give happy hormones a fighting chance.**
Stress hormones have all the advantages, so
we must consciously make the time and
circumstances to let the happy hormones
catch up. Practicing grace means choosing
our reactions rather than deferring to our
animalistic responses. Remember BOBA:
Breathe In, Observe, Breathe Out, Act. We
have to take control of our bodies and emotions
to be able to apply rationality to the situation.
Mindful breathing helps us gain that control.

■ **Take the 35,000-foot view.** Flying in an airplane,
we get a much different perspective from how
we see the world on the ground. We can see
the entire meandering river as opposed to just
one section of it. When we practice grace, we
are less swayed by the heat of the moment. To
prioritize the greater good, we need to take the
broad view so we can account for all factors, not
just what we can see from our vantage point.

■ **Be open to changing your patterns.** Like all the
skills in this book, grace requires that we try to
do things differently than we have done in the
past. If we want to grow, we must be willing
to try new paths. When we try new behaviors
and they feel uncomfortable, we can calm

ourselves by focusing on the greater good. This higher purpose can give us a distraction from our immediate, instinctive response to being uncomfortable. We can't expect the world around us to change if we are unwilling to shift ourselves.

⌃

STEP UP

Grace Challenge:
Create Reminders of Your Higher Purpose

In high-pressure situations, it's easy to become overwhelmed by the intensity and default to stress responses. We see the immediate issue as all consuming rather than as an individual event happening inside a broader picture.

In order to prevent our scope from narrowing, we need constant reminders of the things we believe are most important. One good place to have these reminders is on our devices — as screen savers or other "home base" images.

In the past, I have had photos of my dog, my nieces, and a variety of absurd yet timely cat memes. All of these images ground me. They remind me that no matter what the stress activator is coming through my phone, there are things in my life that motivate me beyond any one incident.

These days, I have a photo of my wife and son on my phone. I may have an impolite, entitled, aggressive email to deal with that elicits a strong desire in me to go head-to-head. But to get into my phone, I have to unlock the screen. To do that, I have to go through a picture of my son. When I see him, my higher purpose instantly snaps back into focus. If he read my agro response, would he be proud of his mama? Stress hormones just can't compete with that.

Where do your stress activators come into your life? What kind of reminders can you place there for yourself to give you that essential pause?

❯❯

PILLAR 5

INDIVIDUALITY

Valuing
What Makes
Us Different

As Americans, we are taught to appreciate individuality. We hear all the time that what makes us unique also makes us strong. Whatever quirk or trait is not valued now will be eventually. It might even be envied by our peers. Popular culture is full of these stories. In fact, we've been hearing them since childhood. Think of the 1964 animated TV special *Rudolph the Red-Nosed Reindeer*, a cartoon that is still broadcast today. Rudolph, one of Santa's reindeer, has a shiny red nose unlike the standard black reindeer nose. At first, he was ostracized and relegated to the Island of Misfit Toys. But given the opportunity to light Santa's way through a storm, Rudolph saved Christmas, won the cute girl reindeer, and got promoted. We watch him go from outcast to hero in a run time of 47 minutes.

Despite this uplifting, all-American tale, the way we view individuality in real life can be quite different. Our quirks are not always celebrated. We don't always find other people's traits endearing, either; in fact, they seem annoying or even threatening. This reaction is not so surprising when we consider that, biologically, we are driven to fear difference. If someone is different from us, they might intend to harm us. They might speak a different language or have a different skin color, a different religion, different habits and tendencies — you name it. Biologically, we believe we need to defend ourselves. This fear is a protective response that causes our stress hormones to spike, flooding our nervous system with cortisol.

We know from the Human Genome Project that human beings are 99.9 percent identical in genetic makeup. Geneticists look at that 0.1 percent difference to try to figure out how diseases develop and how we can maintain our health. But to me, that 0.1 percent difference suggests something else as well: that in spite of the fact that we are more similar than dissimilar, the reptilian part of our brain is on the lookout for friends and foes. Who is like me and who is different from me?

Our instinctive reactions are at the root of our unconscious biases, the unsupported judgments we make in favor of or against others. Of course, we do not always act in a purely primal manner. The rational part of our brain helps to tamp down our knee-jerk fear reactions, allowing us to interact with others even if we also have unconscious misgivings about them. But it takes a little bit of effort and awareness to overcome our instincts. We need to intentionally change how we regard difference.

As everyday leaders, we need to go beyond just tolerating people and things that are unlike us. We must discover the value in individuality and the strength that diversity brings to our collective perspective. But the first step is to acknowledge and appreciate our own individuality. When we do so, we find ways to live as ourselves more out loud in the world. As we become more comfortable in our own skins, we start to value individuality in others, too.

When we look at what makes us distinctive, we might realize that we spend a lot of time hiding our individuality. After Rudolph tried to cover his unique red nose with a black plastic case, he ended up on an isolated island with other outcasts. He was considered defective instead of special. When our uniqueness is not accepted, we might suppress our traits or seek refuge in a place where the judgments are at least less severe. We do this for a variety of reasons, but they are all rooted in self protection and survival.

We can also feel pressure to fit in, to belong to the group, whatever that group is. Sometimes we would just rather be someone else. When I was nine years old, I desperately wanted to be a Notre Dame football player. I was athletic and competitive. I loved sports. I played front-yard football with my dad and uncles every chance I got. Like all good Catholics, our favorite team was Notre Dame. Every year, my dad took my sister and me to South Bend, Indiana, to watch a home game. We had sweatshirts and hats and all the gear. But going to games and tossing a ball on the front lawn was as close as I would ever get to actually playing the game I loved. Girls were not allowed in the local football league.

There was just one day a year when it was possible to imagine that I, too, could be a true player. It's a day when every kid in the country got to be anything they wanted to be — Halloween. But even in make-believe, girls in the eighties were not football players. Girls were cheerleaders. So for three years running, I dressed up as a Notre Dame cheerleader on the last day of October.

I have a great picture of my sister and me from that time. We are both smiling and posing in our costumes, ready to hit the neighborhood and collect our loot. My sister was an ecstatic Strawberry Shortcake. I was right beside her, smiling, wearing my cheerleader makeup and waving my pompoms. But inside, I was disappointed. I didn't want to be a cheerleader. I wanted to be a football player. I still have a visceral reaction to that picture.

Now, I don't have anything against cheerleaders. Cheerleaders are great. My wife was a cheerleader. But to little nine-year old me, a cheerleader was not the female equivalent of a football player.

Even at that young age, I learned that "close enough" didn't really count when it came to individuality. Being a cheerleader didn't satisfy my desire to be a foot-ball player. I was a competitive athlete. I didn't want to be rallying the crowd on the sidelines. By the time I was 12, I wasn't any closer to my desired costume at Halloween, and I wasn't any happier. I was fitting into social norms, including my particular family norms, and it felt smothering.

It was clear to me that if I didn't declare what I really wanted, I'd never get it. My individuality would remain dormant. So I rejected what I considered to be a second-rate role and just switched my costume to Dracula.

Some people might say that my costume switch was a cop-out. They might say that I needed to stay in the fight until I won; I just had to wear down the other side. But anyone with this outlook clearly did not know my mom in the eighties. She was a powerhouse, as glamorous and stylish as actress Farrah Fawcett from the classic TV series *Charlie's Angels*. My mom was also a businesswoman. She owned multiple retail fashion stores in shopping malls across the country. Having her daughter dress as a football player, even one day a year, wasn't exactly her idea of high-power femininity. That wasn't an "acceptable" different. It took me years to realize that her resistance was not her being unaccepting of me. She loved me tremendously, but she was first and foremost and protective mama bear. She would do anything to shield me from what she perceived as the dangers of being different—bullying, ridicule, or social isolation. In reining in my individuality, she was protecting me the best way she knew how.

Just because we see differences, either in ourselves or others, does not mean we value them. In 1979, Henri Tajfel and John Turner devised a theory to explain the psychology of bias and prejudice. They called it social identity theory. It posited that as people, we have a driving need to think highly of ourselves, and to do that, we often choose two primary ways. First, we create a distinctive group that we are part of (the in-group). Secondly, we accentuate the qualities of our group and vilify the qualities of those not in it (the out-group). This division into in-groups and out-groups can be based on the biggest or the slightest distinctions, from race and religion to height and eye color. But even if these distinctions are neutral in themselves, they lay the foundation for assumptions and judgments to grow. We start to see the out-group as more and more different from us. This has a powerful effect on our outlook and behavior, not to mention what we believe is "normal."

All of us have times when we muffle our individuality. Often we do this when we are trying to please people or fit in. I wanted my mom to be happy, even if my go-to outfit was more like my dad's rather than hers. But if we are striving to be more fully ourselves and come out of whatever closet we're in, embracing our own individuality is a crucial step. My switch to the Dracula costume was an attempt to move in that direction.

A friend of mine, who is a veteran, had an experience of suppressing his individuality when he reentered the workforce that perfectly illustrates this point. He retired from the U.S. Army at 38 and wanted to integrate back into civilian life. He had worked reconstructing cities in the Middle East, and during his last 10 years of service, he had been rebuilding infrastructure to distribute clean water. So back home in the United States, he got a job as a water systems expert at an environmental engineering firm. The company advocated on behalf of nonprofits to protect national parks and wildlife from commercial water rights infringement. Although the partners in the firm knew of Tom's military service, he didn't bring it up with his coworkers much. He made an assessment: he decided that he was working with a bunch of tree huggers (the in-group) who were not pro-U.S. military in any way. By extension, they would not be pro-veteran (the out-group).

Tom liked his coworkers and wanted to fit in at his new job, so he kept his previous life with the U.S. Army hidden. He carried the expectation that his colleagues would think less of him if they knew his history. It was a classic case of someone hiding his full personality to protect himself.

But hiding his individuality created an internal rift for him. He was proud of his service. Also, he spent a lot of his time outside of work volunteering with an organization that helped combat veterans to integrate back into life after service. He was passionate about this work. But on Monday mornings when everyone else was talking about their weekends, he kept his mouth shut. He didn't feel that he could truly open up. Imagine going into work every Monday and feeling that you can't risk telling a soul about something that really matters to you, especially when everyone else is talking about their highlights — their kids' soccer game, a concert with friends, a date night, or other volunteer work. It doesn't feel great to be the only one hiding.

One Monday, Tom was particularly exhausted and could not focus at work. Over the weekend, one of the veterans he had been working with had committed suicide. Tom was devastated. Noticing he was not his regular jovial self, his boss called him into her office. He hesitated, but eventually he told her the story. She then shared that three of her family members were currently serving in the armed forces. He was shocked. He'd had no idea his boss had any sort of connection to the military. She also shared with him that other people on the staff had military connections as well. The number of people he could relate to went from zero to ten in a matter of minutes. He also now had at least one person, his boss, who he could speak freely to about his service. Someone who "got it."

The interesting thing is that there were *always* ten people at the company who had a connection to the military. What changed was Tom's perception of his coworkers. Now he knew there were people around him who could understand what his volunteer work meant to him. He took himself out of the perceived out-group and found his in-group. All of that happened because he stopped hiding the fact that he was a veteran and he was passionate about helping others. His life and work outside of the office were just as integral to the person he was as the work he did at his desk every day.

Overwhelmingly, when people tell me their past fears about sharing their individuality, they say they were afraid of being judged and excluded. They then tell me that the fear was not based in reality but rather on something they had created in their head. When Tom became willing to be vulnerable and share a trait of his despite his fears, the result was very positive. He wondered what had taken him so long to take a risk. This is a common story. But we rarely believe it until we are on the other side of our fears. Had we known that the response wouldn't be as negative as we'd anticipated, we would have been more authentically ourselves long ago.

Many of us have been told for years that certain preferences or tendencies are annoying or troublesome or outright unacceptable to others. A perfectionist might hear that their tendency to nitpick every detail can be very irritating. An introvert might get the feedback that they seem antisocial. But what happens when our out-group is not just annoying but made up of the fundamental qualities that we cannot change—for example, when we are not the "right" race or gender? Our difference puts us outside of the mainstream, and we internalize the fear and criticism aimed at us. Then we might even begin to believe the biases ourselves. We downplay our association with the out-group to maintain positive relationships with other people and feel that we have a place in society. But hiding ourselves inevitably creates an internal struggle. And that is unsustainable.

When we examine our individuality, our goal is not to eliminate our contradictions, our annoying characteristics, or traits that other people fear. We can't hide the color of our skin or that we have a physical disability. Our work is to resist the view that our differences are character flaws. These traits are part of who we are. In fact, our individuality shines brightest when we stand out as opposed to blend in. That does not mean we have to be the loudest or the flashiest. It means that we embrace, in ourselves, what makes us unique. Part of our evolution is coming to terms with all of the aspects of our traits and not passing judgment on them. This means all of our attributes—the ones we view as positive or negative as well as the ones society ascribes "good" or "bad" labels to.

At the same time, sometimes we like the traits we have and sometimes we don't. Looking at everything that makes up who we are—the good, the bad, and the ugly—requires a healthy amount of self-compassion. If I am a perfectionist, I am detail-oriented, I am meticulous, and my attention to detail brings great value to any group I'm in. Instead of feeling bad about my meticulousness, I just need to learn how to modulate it. In other words, we need to consider how we affect others in certain contexts. What impact are we making?

As well, we may not feel safe divulging all of our characteristics. If I am afraid to be open about my sexuality in the workplace, for example, I need to practice kindness with myself. My fear is real, and being vulnerable requires a safe environment. But it's also true that if I feel isolated at work, I will also feel alienated there. I want to find friends and allies, not hide myself away. So I have to find and create my social support system at my job. This may start with one person, but my willingness to share my individuality empowers my allies to help me through this process. It allows allies to *be* allies.

Bottom line: we need to find the positive in our traits, acknowledge the potential or perceived negatives, and figure out how to interact with our community. In other words, we need to embrace our individuality and recognize where potential biases may arise. This awareness empowers us to be functional in any given situation.

To me, the ultimate external expression of individuality is dancing. For years, I thought I was a terrible dancer. I absolutely loved music, but I hated dancing. In fact, it still makes me uncomfortable. I was so afraid of other people's judgments that I avoided it altogether. My self-consciousness made me so uptight that I stiffened up on the dance floor, making matters worse. I wouldn't even dance in the living room with my nieces. It was a vicious, rhythmless, downward spiral.

But then I went to a music festival and saw other people dancing. Sure, some of them were great, but most people were just average, and a few of them were "bad." What made me appreciate them is that it didn't really matter how well or badly they danced, they were just being themselves. Am I the first person to run out onto the dance floor today? Not at all. But I am pushing myself into situations where I do the uncomfortable thing in order to be more comfortable with it. Through this process, I've realized that, actually, no one is watching me dance. There are many more things to pay attention to besides me. And if people judge me, I'm okay with it. I'm enjoying the music, and I'm enjoying myself.

Once we have embraced our own individuality and find the joy and flexibility in expressing it, it becomes possible to be more accepting of others' individuality too. We are less afraid of being judged or excluded, so some part of us relaxes and becomes more open to the uniqueness of others too. We are less likely to create in-groups and out-groups because we actually see the value in difference. We start to see assets where before we might have seen threats or deficits. We see differences as interesting, from the very obvious ones such as height, weight, gender, and race, to the more nuanced such as style, personality, and life choices. This outlook helps us to overcome our psychologically driven fear of difference and to consciously choose to be curious over being fearful and judgmental.

Embracing the individuality of others, as well as our own, is a vital part of stepping up. It does not serve our organization, our family, or our community to only associate with people who look like us and act like us. It may be tempting because it seems safe. But it is also boring and myopic. The best ideas and situations that promote growth come from associating with the most diverse people. It also helps us to practice other pillars of leadership, such as empathy, grace, and humility, because it so dramatically expands the scope of what we're curious about.

Prioritizing everyone's individuality is the difference between being a role model and being a leader. A role model is someone who fully and unabashedly lives their individuality out loud. We all need role models. We can become role models ourselves. But leaders not only live their own individuality out loud, they also create environments that encourage others to do so as well.

« Takeaways »

■ **Recognize that we are hardwired for fear.** We are psychologically predisposed to fear difference. It's natural. It is important to be aware of when we are creating in-groups and out-groups. We can be more inclusive when we are aware of when we make distinctions based on assumptions or unconscious biases.

■ **Embrace difference.** We all have traits, characteristics, and markers of difference. Some we come into life with, while others get established over time. Some we want to hide because the outside world fears them or simply because we don't like them. But by hiding or minimizing our individuality to avoid disapproval or rejection, we tamp down who we truly are. By accepting our individuality rather than being ashamed of it or distancing ourselves from it, we can figure out how we can best integrate our genuine selves into our daily interactions.

■ **Be a leader in how you react.** It is undeniable that others have found some of our characteristics troublesome or fear-inducing. If my gender expression is problematic to some people, then that perception is a fact to them. That is their reality, and denying it exists is meaningless. The way I approach our interaction is what sets me apart. Am I defensive and confrontational, or am I open and engaging? I can't control someone else's reaction. I can only control how I handle it.

■ **Acknowledge that our individuality has strengths and challenges.** If we are told only the bad things about our characteristics, we need to acknowledge for ourselves that there is strength in them too. Often the things that isolate us make us more resilient in the long run. Those traits also allow us to find empathy for others who experience similar social exile.

≫

STEP UP
Individuality Challenge:
Examine Your Implicit Bias

We all have implicit bias. Simply by being a human on this earth, we observe, analyze, and categorize the world around us. Having implicit bias does not make you a racist or a sexist, it means that your brain is trying to organize the complex world that we live in. But it is critical that we are aware of our biases and how they affect our actions and perceptions of the world.

Next time you have an interaction with someone that bothers you, look at why you were bothered. Make a list of the first things that come to your mind. Then, a few hours later when your aggravation has lessened, make a list of all of the traits of that person both demographic (age, gender, race, religion, etc.) and personal (rude, entitled, aloof, condescending, uneducated, etc.). What connections do you make between these traits without even thinking? Was the interaction actually condescending, or do you think that because the other person was older than you or seemed more privileged (or less privileged) than you? Do you assume a level of expertise or ignorance based on race or gender?

It is not an easy process to look at our unconscious biases. We do not want to see what they reveal about ourselves. But they work in a more positive direction: I might give the benefit of the doubt to someone who has similar traits to me (say, another lesbian) because our shared experience gives her instant credibility. This is also a bias, but it doesn't feel as bad.

Implicit bias is pervasive. We all have it. Becoming aware that it exists and of how it impacts our decisions help us to step up. We can't change what we are unaware of, but once we are aware, we have the power to change.

≫

PILLAR 6

HUMILITY

*Checking
Your Ego
at the Door*

Once we start valuing individuality, we have a lot more skill and potential to work with both in ourselves and in others. We're not hiding our own interests and tendencies, and we're not judging others' quirks and characteristics as weaknesses. We start seeing strengths everywhere. This is a very helpful and powerful change in perspective. It can be exhilarating. It can even feel liberating. But sometimes, along with this new confidence can also come arrogance. We may have the best of intentions, but our ego may also start getting in our way.

No matter how epic and transformative our journey is, it is simply that—a discovery of our *own* selves. Everyone's journey is different. It is not our job to tell other people what the righteous path looks like. It is more important to inspire them to find their own path. To superimpose my experience on someone else in order to show them "the way," even if I have the best intentions, negates their individuality. We must allow others to grow and self-define in their own time and in their own way. In other words, we need to allow others to discover their fullest and bravest selves for themselves. To let people have their own process and their own timing is an act of respect and humility.

When we have more confidence and a stronger sense of self, there's always the danger of becoming self-important. For me, once I finally came out as gay, I experienced tremendous relief and empowerment. I immediately started to believe that anyone who knew they were gay should come busting out of their closets, too, preferably draped in rainbows and glitter. I couldn't understand why they weren't. Life was so much better out of the closet! I was so enthusiastic about this change in my life that I actually started judging people who had not yet come out. The fact that just weeks previously, I had been in their exact position was totally lost on me. I had no perspective on where I'd just come from. I was only looking forward. But I needed to also look back and keep in mind that I was not so different from those people I was judging.

After years of feeling disempowered, it was thrilling to feel more valued, and in a very public way. In 2013, I did my first TEDx Talk, "Coming Out of Your Closet," and it went viral just like my Ignite talk had. I had started 2013 speaking at middle schools and local community organizations. But by that fall, I was speaking at Harvard. Life had become a whirlwind and I was just trying to keep up. In fact, I had no idea what I was doing. I spent half my time creating content for my keynotes and the other half of the time convincing myself I deserved to take those stages. It was *fake it until you make it* in its purest sense. My ego needed to catch up and help me believe I was worthy of talking to all these people.

On the positive side of things, I was starting to see that my keynotes were having a significant impact. I was proud of that. People believed in what I had to say, and I was starting to believe in it too. My new pride also allowed me to be more open to interactions with anyone who approached me. The downside was that it also started clouding my vision.

As my personal pendulum swung toward confidence, I began to crave the recognition. I was enjoying my new viral celebrity a bit too much. In the fall of 2014, about a year after the TEDx video was released, I was at one of my "real" jobs working as a contractor for a trade show. I had just wrapped up a speaking tour at Southern California community colleges. It was a quick transition from being on stage in front of an audience that was eager to hear what I had to say to driving a forklift around a convention center. I loved both roles (and needed both since my speaking career still did not pay all the bills). One just fed my ego more.

At the end of one particularly long work day, I went to meet up with some friends for happy hour. Scanning the bar for them, I made eye contact with a group of people in the corner. They were pointing and whispering to each other, and from where I stood, it looked like they were waving me over. I figured they recognized me from my videos and wanted to chat or take a selfie. I had not seen my friends yet, so I had time. I made my way over.

"Hi, I noticed you were staring," I said. Before they could say anything, I added, "I wanted you to know that yes, it's me, Ash Beckham." They stared blankly.

"You know, Ash, from the YouTube videos."

Nothing.

"It's me, it's Ash. You know, 'Coming Out of Your Closet?' I am probably trending on your Facebook feed right now!"

"I don't know what you are talking about," one of the women said when I finally paused to take a breath. "We were just waving you over to get us a drink. Don't you work here?"

Awkward silence.

It turned out I was wearing the exact same blue button-down shirt and black pants as the banquet staff. I laughed sheepishly. I offered to buy them a round of drinks as an apology for my foolish mistake. They accepted. When I returned with the drinks, I explained what I was talking about—my TEDx Talk had recently gone viral, and people were recognizing me everywhere I went. The people at the table certainly had a lot of questions about the whole TED Talk process. It ended up being a decent conversation. Was it a victory or a defeat? Like most awkward interactions, it was a draw. It was a victory in that, despite my embarrassment, I did not just tuck tail and run. I found an opportunity to connect with this group of strangers. They learned a little bit more about me, and I learned a little bit more about them.

There was certainly defeat in there as well. My embarrassment came from realizing that I was assuming I was a celebrity everywhere I went and that my impact was larger than it actually was. Fueled by how often I was being told that my talks were meaningful, I'd begun to believe that everyone must be seeing them.

This interaction was an abrupt and painful reality check. But it was an entirely necessary one. During that first rush of celebrity and success, I had no idea what was happening or what my ego was doing. In fact, when we begin to experience success and receive positive feedback, a lot of dopamine gets released in our brain. It feels good, so of course we crave more. We prioritize success (or perceived success) over humility. But after too many painfully awkward incidents — diva moments when I was doing too much talking and not enough listening — I realized that my ego was getting in the way of my ability to connect with others. I had to check myself.

Despite my temporary celebrity and relative success, the scope of my impact was much smaller than my ego perceived it to be. I had to consciously combat my brain's desire for more dopamine. Over time, I realized that my true power lay in being a real, fallible human rather than someone whose messages were edited for mass distribution on YouTube. It was in humility, not pride, that I was able to connect with other people. When they realized that I was just your average lesbian next door, someone who had become an advocate by accident, it helped them to open up. It made their own path to advocacy seem much more appealing and plausible. I slowly realized that, like any skill, we get better at humility the more we try to embrace it. Today, I know how to recognize when my ego is getting the upper hand.

Humility and ego are like opposite sides of a balancing scale. What we are striving for is equilibrium — the perfect balance in the center. When we have successes or we begin to value our individuality more, our scale tips toward ego. We feel proud of ourselves. We feel like we might be as special as we always hoped. We wonder if we are better than others. On the other hand, if we overcorrect our ego, we risk putting ourselves down and minimizing our true strengths. Self-deprecation is not the same as humility. Humility is not playing down who we are. It is not beating ourselves up or doing the humble brag. It is acknowledging our strengths and being aware of where they fit into the world outside our own bubbles where we feel safest.

When we are learning and growing, it can feel like we're swinging between confidence and modesty, like we're a pinball bouncing back and forth from bumper to bumper. The goal is not to get better at tolerating the violent bouncing. The goal is to make the overall amount of bouncing less to find plumb. It's a process.

There are many ways to find that balance between overvaluing and undervaluing ourselves. One way is to understand that we are simultaneously a mentee and a mentor. In other words, throughout our lives, we are always simultaneously someone's student and someone's teacher. If we really look, we will always find people we can look up to who inspire us to be our best selves. These are our mentors. If we have a personal relationship with them, we confide in them and grow under their guidance. But we don't even have to know our mentors personally for them to make an impact on us. Simply reading the writings of people we admire — whether it's Gandhi or Maya Angelou or Harvey Milk or someone else — can inspire us to live our lives with higher values, strive to affect our communities in more positive ways, and understand that we are not the first or the last person doing what we're doing.

At the same time, we are always someone's teacher, the person to whom others look for inspiration and guidance. We are just a bit further down the path than they are. Let's say I am part of a local organization that wants to make positive environmental change locally. One of our initiatives is increasing awareness about the impact of plastic bags in our community. I have volunteered to work our booth at the local farmers market to talk to people about our mission. I am just a volunteer with no official role in the organization, but I am well-informed about the issues and feel comfortable speaking to others about them. When I show up to the market for my shift, another volunteer joins me who believes just as passionately as I do about the problem. But he is just beginning his advocacy and has never discussed the issue in depth before. All of a sudden I have the opportunity to mentor him. He is eager to learn, and I am willing to share. A mentor–mentee relationship can be as simple and informal as that.

Another way to practice humility is to let go of status and attachment to things that represent status — or at least to take a good look at these things. My mom often told the story of my dad buying his first car out of college, a '65 Corvette. When people asked him what he drove, he would always say a Chevy. Technically, that was true, since Chevrolet is the manufacturer of the Corvette. But it wasn't the whole truth.

My dad, like a lot of men in the sixties, liked sports cars. This was before the time of luxury imports, so if you were a sports-car guy, the Corvette was the top of the line. It looked like nothing else on the road. It looked like a racecar. He loved owning it but didn't want to brag about driving one of the nicest cars of the era. When my dad would modestly answer that he drove a Chevy, it would make my mom crazy. "You worked two jobs throughout college to afford that car. Why won't you tell people you drive a Corvette?"

My dad's response was that anyone who knew him knew he drove a Corvette. He did not want to appear pretentious to anyone who didn't know him. If people eventually found out the truth, fine. If they didn't, that was fine also. If someone thought he actually drove a Chevy, it didn't bother him one bit. It was critical to him to seem approachable and on a level with anyone he met.

For most of us, our default inclination is to strive for external markers of success, not to cultivate humility.

When we start to get a little bit of power, it's easy to become dependent on it to justify our authority or expertise. We measure our worth based on the things we possess, whether they are material like a car or immaterial like a job title or the number of social media followers we have. We value *things* more than connection, and this begins to cloud our judgment. Those material things we strive for are only relevant externally. Are we going for the designer purse or the fancy position or the number of clicks and likes because these are things internally valuable to us or because they convey status to ourselves and others? A humble life isn't necessarily meager, just as a life of status isn't necessarily rich. How would it impact us if we did not attain these specific status symbols? Do we have less value as human beings if we drive a Toyota rather than a Mercedes? In other words, are we externally or internally motivated to achieve the status we're going for?

When we cultivate humility, we remove the pressure to constantly strive to impress others. Our values shift. What becomes important to us is not how expensive the dinner table is but rather our connection to the people who sit around it. We become invested in immaterial successes — strong friendships, integration into our community, the pursuit of our passions. Connection and relationships begin to feel much more important than possessions.

Practicing humility often means we actively find and create situations that call for it. Do we volunteer at the local school? Do we help out our neighbors in times of need? Do we hold the door for strangers? How do we contribute to the greater good? It is not solely dictated by our net worth. Sure, the more money we have, perhaps the more we can give back or the more time we have to help out. But as everyday leaders, our value as people is no greater if we can write a check for a million dollars or if we get up early to clean a neighborhood park before work.

Mother Teresa, for example, made a point of showing that there was no work that was beneath her. Her life's work was to care for others. But if you asked her what her greatest accomplishment was, she would say she was an expert toilet cleaner. Cleaning toilets is one of the least desirable jobs going. But even after she had received the Nobel Peace Prize and had opened 62 homes for the dying poor, she would spend most Sundays at one of the homes cleaning the toilets and emptying the bedpans of the sick. Certainly, she had the power and the authority to request that any other staff member do that job. But practicing humility was part of her daily work.

We don't need to go around cleaning toilets to show that we are humble. Situations exist every day that give us a chance to practice. Some just show up in front of us and some we have to create. We do not have to make big gestures. Humility can happen in very small ways. Just because it is simple doesn't mean it is easy. We can let the person in the grocery store with one item step in front of us. We can hold the door for people with no expectation of a thank-you. We can own up to our losing our temper with our kids. Excuses and justifications for our actions come to mind easily, and even when we try, we are not going to get humility right every time. But practicing humility means being accountable for our actions and striving to be better the next time.

The ego might put up a fight against cultivating humility because the craving for dopamine can be strong. Dopamine contributes to feelings of pleasure and satisfaction that the ego can't resist. It wants it all and it wants it now. The ego does not worry about consequences or the big picture. It worries about immediacy and itself. That intense desire comes on fast, but if we can outlast it and keep checking in with ourselves, we can make that situation an opportunity to grow.

« Takeaways »

■ **Remember the past.** Remembering where we've come from helps us to have compassion for those who are at different stages of their journey. Our impulse can be to distance ourselves from our past as a sign of progress. But in doing so, we minimize both where we come from and the people who are still in that place. It prevents us from having compassion and being a resource to others.

■ **Do a status check.** When we truly practice humility, we can take a good look at our attachment to status. What external things represent status to you? How attached are you to these things? Why? What are you afraid will happen if you lose that status or status item? When we become aware of the external things we are clinging to, we have more opportunity to discover our internal sense of what we *really* value. Practice humility with yourself first and then try it out in your relationships with others.

- **Admit when you are wrong.** We are going to make mistakes. Everyone does, but not everyone admits it. In our humility practice, there is no need to justify mistakes or make excuses to deny fault. If you messed up, own it, fix it (if possible), and move on. Do the next right thing. Avoiding responsibility and displacing blame destroys trust.

⌃

STEP UP
Humility Challenge:
Take a Back Seat Next Time

We are in situations every day in which we need to make a final decision. That could be deciding on a budget at work or deciding what to buy at the grocery store to feed our family. Humility requires us to relinquish some control. It is the willingness to be open to other possibilities. An attitude of humility sets the stage for honest, collaborative, and transparent interactions.

If you feel like you are always calling all the shots, experiment with letting someone else make the decisions the next time you have a low-risk opportunity to let go of the reins. Low risk does not mean there is zero chance of failure. There must be some risk of "failure" for it to be an opportunity for growth. I mean that the consequences will be minimal if someone does things differently than you would.

Here is a simple example. Children give us abundant chances to practice humility. If I am visiting my nieces and they want to cook a meal, I don't just boss them around the kitchen. I feel like I'm a pretty good cook, but I put that aside. My job is to guide them. I allow them to pick the recipe, assemble the ingredients, and go through the process of preparing the meal. I let them have an experience for the purpose of empowering them to do something they have never tried before.

My role is not to execute but to oversee, to put up the guardrails rather than drive the car. I don't let them have unsupervised access to the knives in the house, but I also don't forbid them from using the stove, as long as I am nearby. This can sometimes be really hard, but it gives us the opportunity to grow. I might end up eating overcooked spaghetti and a strange tomato sauce for dinner, but the smiles on their faces and the empowerment they feel from their creation will make it a little more palatable.

⏬

PILLAR 7

PATIENCE

Learning to Take a Pause

n our world of instant gratification, patience is a lost art. It takes time to develop courage, grace, humility, empathy, and so on. It even takes time to simply realize what we are experiencing and which tool to use in which situation. But the world around us has no time for patience.

A lot of this is because all the information we could ever want is in the smartphones in our pockets. We can play one of millions of songs instantly just by asking our devices. We can make it happen with our voice — we don't even need the inconvenience of touching a screen. We get alerts about breaking news constantly, whether it is from a world leader or our best friend from third grade. We can even stay connected while flying through the sky in a welded chunk of metal. We don't have to wait for anything. If we are delayed in the grocery store because the person in front of us can't use the self-scanner with expert efficiency, it seems like a travesty. We become extremely frustrated when the most recent cat video takes a moment to buffer.

In this amped-up environment, we expect our own capacity to make decisions to be just as instant, even if we're under a lot of pressure. And we expect these to be *good* decisions. But our brains don't work best that way. There are two areas of our brains that are in battle: the emotional and the logical parts. The emotional part is fed by dopamine — that feel-good brain hormone that I mentioned in the previous chapter. We see the piece of cake, and we want it *now*. This impulse served our ancestors years ago when they did not know when they would get their next meal. But these days, we have the luxury of allowing the logical part of our brain to have a say in our situations. For example, if we are watching what we eat and have a choice of snack options, we know that an apple would be a healthy choice. It obviously has better long-term outcomes. But if the cake is available, that's what we reach for. It's as if we have an angel and a devil sitting on our shoulders.

Which part of our brain wins depends on the situation. Researchers at Princeton University concluded that when we get really close to obtaining a reward, the emotional part of our brain takes over, and we prioritize instant gratification. For example, if the cake is on the counter as opposed to at the store down the street, the emotional brain is in high gear. It does not care about future consequences.

It wants the cake. With the cake right in front of us, there's nothing in the way of us having it except for our logic.

The way to counter the selfish and hedonistic impulses of our emotional brains is to outlast temptation. To do this, we practice the critical skill of patience. We consciously take time to let the logical part of our brain, which thinks about our future, catch up and bring reason to the situation. Patience with ourselves and others gives us a split second to reflect and ensure we are being proactive instead of reactive. The cake still looks really tasty, but (on a good day) we remember our commitment to eat better and choose the apple instead.

Patience is the ability to allow some space for thoughts, ideas, or situations to unfold a little instead of rushing into action with our first impulse. Often, successful people are celebrated and promoted to positions of leadership because they are nimble thinkers and action takers. This can certainly be a strength. Organizations must be led by people who are willing to act. But always rushing to make *fast* decisions can also be a weakness. When we feel this kind of pressure, the quality of our thinking can decrease, and we can rush into risky situations.

Patience helps ensure that we make decisions and actions with a calm, clear mind that keeps the larger picture in sight. It is a balance between our ability to think quickly and our ability to consider many things beyond our immediate concerns, and to be deliberate in our choices.

For ten years, my dad and I ran a girls' fastpitch softball tournament company together. My dad was the visionary and the steady hand. He dreamed big, and I was the task-oriented person who attempted to actualize those dreams. We made an incredible team. In our line of work, the fastpitch teams expected immediate answers. Our biggest challenge was rain. The moment the drops started falling, the questions would start. Would we make up the games? When would they be played? What field? When would we know? What if it rained more? What if it stopped? The pressure that came from our customers was rooted in a need for instant information. It was simultaneously understandable and ridiculous.

Answers depended on several unknowable factors: how long it would rain, how much it would rain, when would it rain again, etc. We could never know anything with any certainty. No one could! Despite this, people still wanted to know the plan. What I wanted to say was, "If I could control the weather, I would certainly use my skills somewhere more lucrative than softball tournaments." But we were a customer-service organization, so I bit my tongue.

Even if our options were unknowable, I always thought that we might as well guess at answers so we could tell the teams *something*. My dad didn't see things that way. In fact, although he and I worked in sync nearly flawlessly, this was one of our sticking points. I felt that he made decisions too slowly. Once the rain stopped, we would need teams on the fields immediately, and they needed enough time to get to those fields, wherever they might be. We could not let a team know at 4:45 p.m. that their start time was 5:00 p.m. They could be at lunch or back at their hotels. They weren't going to sit around in the rain waiting to play. The pressure was on.

It pained me how deliberate and calculated my dad was in making these decisions. It took so much time. But what we lost in time was always balanced by a final decision that was more thoughtful and inclusive. He always took the panoramic perspective. He made the decision based on what outcome would be the most beneficial for the largest number of teams. He didn't play to the squeaky wheel. He empathized with their desire to advocate for the best interests of their team, but he also took into consideration the interests of the teams who had respect for what we were doing and were patiently awaiting our decisions.

Patience, it turns out, is the ability to recognize both external and internal pressures and make balanced decisions in spite of their influences.

That external pressure made me want to come up with answers as quickly as possible. I was more concerned about the speed of my response than with the accuracy of it—a classic case of impatience. I did not think about future consequences but allowed the emotional part of my brain to have the final say. I just wanted these people off our backs.

After my dad passed away in November 2017, I did not have his careful consideration to counterbalance my natural instinct to act and decide quickly. I had incredible people in my event team helping us continue to run the tournaments, but none of them had the patience he had. Especially not me. Since I was now the person with the most experience, I became the one calling a lot of the shots. We made decisions very fast, which was well received in the beginning. But as the season went on, we made more and more bad decisions that would then have to be adjusted multiple times because I had not taken into account all of the factors. I was also listening to the squeaky wheels so that some of our decisions were biased toward one particular team or another. People were frustrated. It was understandable.

About two-thirds of the way through the season, I could see that my quick-fire decision making was giving me more headaches than resolutions. We were having to refund money and make dozens of individual phone calls to coordinate schedules rather than getting it right from the start. We were apologizing over and over for our mistakes.

On reflection, I could see that some of these problems could have been avoided if I had just taken a little more time in deciding. I had to somehow learn how to maintain a sense of urgency while also factoring in as many variables as possible. I also needed to understand what the coaches really wanted. They were getting as many questions from parents as I was getting from them. They just wanted to pass on something.

People were frustrated, but they were also reasonable, for the most part. They knew I didn't control the weather, yet they needed predictability. Leaving people in the dark while I agonized over decisions was not an effective leadership strategy either. So everyone in our organization started to communicate to our teams differently. We became very honest and forthcoming when we needed to hit the pause button.

The key, I realized, is that pause, that moment of patience.

Patience sometimes has negative connotations and is equated with passivity. But it is far from passive. To be patient is not to be inert or inactive. We were still actively making decisions, communicating, and monitoring the situation. But we weren't rushing or forcing anything. Patience allows for the time to make the *best* call and to come up with better processes if those are needed. We aren't less efficient, we're actually more efficient. We make fewer mistakes, require fewer revisions of our decisions, and lead ourselves and others astray a lot less often.

Our patience or impatience sets the tone for how we interact with our environment every day. For me, a scenario that constantly challenges my patience is being in traffic — specifically, merging. I dread it. It's a situation in which multiple people are jockeying to get to the same place at the same time with no objective arbiter to say who *truly* was first.

Now, imagine merging in a construction zone. Two lanes have become one. We see many giant arrows and the orange cones telling us this. It is obvious that the lane ahead is closed. But there is always some driver who speeds by everyone and nudges in at the head of the line. My first reaction is pure anger. Who does this guy think he is? Why does he believe he is more important than the rest of us? He may think he can cut in front of these other folks, but he is definitely not cutting in front of me. My stress hormones rage. I believe in a fair and just society, and this guy has just become a major threat to that.

But I am committed to stepping up. So I try to bring patience with me even in the most exasperating situations. I entertain alternative narratives to the one I have created in my head. What if this guy was rushing to the hospital? If that was the case, I would certainly let him in. Since I will never know the full story, it's just a matter of what I want to believe.

More importantly, it is about who I want to be. Would I rather be the person who assumes the worst in everyone in order to protect herself and her pride? Or would I rather be the person who gave people the benefit of the doubt?

This intention to practice patience with ourselves and others keeps our stress hormones in check and allows our happy hormones to flow. After all, it takes a lot of energy to actively engage in conflict and justify my righteous position so I can fume about the arrogant jerk I assume someone is.

But when I give this guy the benefit of the doubt, I sidestep all my stress responses and concerns. What does it cost me to give him a break? Not much. And if he is having a really bad day, then I could be the one giving him the break he needs. Everyone could use a little patience from strangers from time to time.

In the vast majority of life's situations, there is middle ground between taking a hard position and being a pushover. When we are quick to react, we don't give situations any time to evolve or resolve. Patience gives us the chance to find that middle ground and even, perhaps, a solution that satisfies multiple interests. This is very helpful, especially as we feel ourselves getting amped up and reactive.

We have lots of opportunities to practice patience in our most cherished relationships. These could be with a spouse or child or with a parent or close friend. We love them dearly, and yet sometimes they drive us crazy. Who hasn't been in conflict with a loved one at some point? But practicing patience with these folks is lowest risk and highest yield. They are the ones most likely not to abandon us if we get impatient, yet they are also the most likely to value the extra attention.

At a coffee shop recently, I witnessed an incredible display of patience between a mom and her toddler. They were talking and joking with each other in a cute way that caught my attention. Then, for seemingly no reason, the toddler had a meltdown. In an instant, she was lying in the middle of the café, pounding her fists and stomping her feet. It was a full-on tantrum. The mom was calm yet calculated. She immediately took her daughter outside to the empty patio. She was not losing her marbles in an otherwise stressful situation. I was mesmerized.

At first, the woman held her daughter until she stopped sobbing. Then she squatted down to her child's level so they were eye to eye. She didn't break eye contact with her child, and she didn't say anything. She just kept nodding and smiling.

After a full 2 minutes of nodding, the mom started talking. I couldn't hear her tone because she was outside, but her face did not show anger or frustration. When they walked back into the café, I was staring: I had to see how round two would go. The toddler was still whimpering, but she kept herself together. Her mom ordered their beverages and snacks, and they took a seat. I had seen hundreds of meltdowns but never such a reasonable resolution.

"I have to ask, what did you do?" I asked. I had to know this mom's secret. "Do you have some superpower that allows you to rationalize with toddlers?!" She laughed and told me her approach. First, take a break. Remove yourselves from the situation, temporarily if possible rather than permanently. She always tried to give her toddler a second chance. If they just left the coffee shop, no one got what they wanted.

Once removed, she let her toddler try to explain why she was upset. Instead of guessing what was setting her daughter off or what would fix it, she listened. In this case, her daughter didn't like the shoes she'd decided to wear. She had on sneakers but wanted the sparkle shoes, which were at home. Wanting those shoes had suddenly become too much to bear. Her mom could have made a hundred guesses and never have come close to understanding what was going on. Taking the time to let her child talk saved that mom a lot of time and aggravation. She got a more accurate read on the situation, which helped her to soothe her child. And she got her latte.

Not all of us deal with toddlers, but we all deal with some level of conflict in our lives. Practicing patience in the heat of the moment can relieve that stress and deescalate fraught situations. Letting people talk can change a tense dynamic for the better, giving us a better chance of finding a solution or at least a middle ground. Sometimes we don't have to jump in and fix things, we just need to listen. Solutions can come in the process of patiently paying attention.

Practicing patience can also take the form of creating an intentional pause. That can manifest in a variety of ways. Sometimes you need to just walk away. We can completely remove ourselves from a situation and take a solo walk around the block or table a conversation for a later time when tempers have cooled. That intentional pause can also mean pulling someone aside to address the conflict privately so that it does not blow up publicly. A pause can also be as simple and short as the split second it takes for a deep breath. The exact time frame and logistics are much less important than conscious and calculated effort to interrupt the current situation and insert some space.

Beyond relieving immediate stress, patience gives us the room to practice the other ideas we discuss in this book. When I take the time to actually listen to someone else, it empowers me to be more empathetic. If I take a pause and walk away to get some big picture, I can tap in to grace and humility. To do this, I must be patient with myself as well. When we are learning new skills like these, we need to give ourselves room to be awkward and unskillful at first. Changing our behavior is not going to happen immediately. We need time to evolve into the people we want to be.

We have opportunities to practice patience every single day and in every interaction. The scenarios are endless. But the rewards are immediate. We can see the difference in our relationships and in our physiology right away. Patience is one of the easiest skill to practice, but as we all know, it can be one of the hardest to slow down and master.

« Takeaways »

- **Notice the external pressures.** Much of our drive to make quick decisions comes from external pressures — timelines, demands from other people, the need for instant information. It can be overwhelming and can push us to a state of reactivity rather than thoughtful action. The more we are aware of these pressures, the easier it is to disentangle ourselves and prioritize patience.

- **Distinguish between patience and inaction.** Patience does not require that we sit on our hands and watch the world go by. The kind of patience we are talking about can be a split-second pause. We all need to make decisions, just not necessarily as fast as the world has us believe.

- **Increase your efficiency.** Sometimes our rationale for making immediate decisions is the time crunch we are under. But in reality, the amount of time it takes to pause in the moment is more than made up for by the mistakes we prevent in the long run.

- **Leave room for better resolution.** This one touches on humility too. Often, we take control of a situation because we believe we should. But if we step back momentarily and let the situation run its natural course, we might realize a better solution.

⌃

STEP UP
Patience Challenge:
Intentionally Insert a Pause

Patience takes practice. It takes the conscious decision to slow down. Next time you find yourself in a high-pressure situation where you are making a decision, stop for 30 seconds. In that time, consider any factors you may be overlooking. Who else will be impacted? Do you *need* to insert yourself into the situation? What are some alternative courses of action that you can take? Be sure to also take a deep breath.

The purpose of practicing patience is not necessarily to come to a different answer than what your gut is telling you. The point is to take the time to consider solutions that are not necessarily right in front of you. This allows you to make the best decision possible for everyone, including yourself.

⌄

AUTHENTICITY

Coming into Alignment

These days, authenticity is quite a buzzword. It's on magazine covers and all over self-help blogs. How many times have you read, "Ten steps to a more authentic life," or, "eight traits of authentic people"? But authenticity is not a checklist, and it's not a destination. It is not a badge we earn or a status we claim. It's not a one-and-done kind of deal. Authenticity is a practice we do every day to be both the person we truly are and to become the person we strive to be.

I arrived at this realization through a painful loss.

My day started with a frantic trip to IKEA. Is there really any other kind? I went to get an end table and a shower caddy but walked out with a sectional couch. On my way home, bouncing down the highway, back hatch open, bungee cords barely holding everything in the car, I called my parents to catch up.

It was a very typical conversation. I talked to my mom about the places they had been eating on their vacation. I talked to my dad about our girls' fastpitch softball tournaments we ran together. As I pulled into my driveway, my dad and I wrapped up and said goodbye, but not "I love you." It is a point of pride as a family that we end every call with "I love you." If we don't, then we call back just to say it. I always did. Every time. But this time, I had half a couch out of my car and places to go, so I didn't call back. A few hours later, after the couch had been assembled (with the use of a hammer that was not listed in the directions), I got a call from my mom. My dad had had an aneurysm.

Over the next week, my dad fought hard to stay alive. But day after day, he never regained consciousness. Seven days later, he passed. We never spoke again.

You can imagine my devastation. As any healthy neurotic would, I beat myself up going over how I had messed up. I always call back. Why didn't I call back? I took the lesson to be — *always F*#KING call back!*

I spent the better part of the next month obsessively calling people back. I'd call my mom back if we didn't say we loved each other an equal number of times. I'd call my sister back in case one of my nieces had forgotten to tell me something. I'd call my wife back to make sure she really, *really* wanted pasta for dinner. I was even trying to call telemarketers back to make sure they were clear I wasn't interested.

Clearly, grief and shock had made me a little bit out of whack. Then, on a work trip, I checked into a hotel and the keycard for my room had these words printed on it: *It's time to let me go.* (The hotel was announcing a new app that would soon replace keycards.) Grief and the universe have a sick and twisted relationship. It was clearly a sign. But then I heard my dad's voice, clear as day: "The lesson is not to call back, Ash. Sometimes you just can't call back. The lesson is to make sure the people you love *know* you love them so that you don't need to call back."

In an instant, my perspective changed. It *was* a sign — not to let my dad go but to let go of my obsessive behavior and be at peace knowing I loved my dad and he knew very well that I did. In that relationship, I was practicing authenticity.

In the most basic sense, authenticity means how we *see* ourselves (internal self) is in alignment with how we *behave* (external self). I saw myself as a loving daughter; I always said, *I love you.* It may sound simple, but there are powerful triggers everywhere that seem to be waiting to force us out of alignment. They compel us to act against our values or resolutions or to not act at all. But in my relationship with my dad, I was in alignment. And I knew what authenticity *felt* like.

The triggers may be intense, but we always know when we are out of alignment. We can feel it in our gut. It's that queasy feeling that signals dread, guilt, fear — whatever it is. We know who we are striving to be — an ally, friend, advocate, educator — but for some reason our behavior does not (or cannot, depending on the situation) reflect that internal vision of ourselves. The practice of living authentically is getting those two parts of ourselves on the same page.

For me, the disconnect has a noise. It sometimes is an internal voice that questions my action or inaction. At other times it sounds like the noise on the *Family Feud* game show when the big red X shows up on the screen. When I am repeatedly out of alignment, that noise becomes too loud to ignore. Something has to give.

It is important to note that authenticity does not always mean changing our behavior to meet the expectation of who we are *in our heads*. We sometimes have to change our expectations. If I consider myself an ally but don't behave like one, I have two options. I can change my behavior to get into alignment, or I can change my expectations of myself to be more in line with my behavior. One option may seem better than the other, but both are authentic.

If you've read this far in the book, you know that I try to embody and enact all the qualities of stepping up that I'm talking about: empathy, courage, grace, humility, individuality, and so on. But sometimes, even today, my less-than-ideal tendencies return and take me by surprise. They always create learning opportunities, but they are also very, very uncomfortable. Just because we have stepped up doesn't mean we are immune to any future challenges or conflict, especially from inside ourselves.

Here's an example. In spite of my resolve to be a compassionate agent for change, in the fall of 2016 I found myself at the center of an escalating situation. I was a guest speaker at a rural state college. After the event, I was outside on the quad talking with some students about LGBTQ issues on campus. A couple of guys walked by. Let's call them Sweatshirt Guy and Backward-Hat Guy. Seeing the group's rainbow flag, one of them shouted, "You know, the Bible says Adam and *Eve* not Adam and *Steve!*"

The group of students I was with immediately started to react. A few puffed out their chests and prepared to shout back, but most slunk down and pulled out their phones to avoid eye contact. They were reacting from the reptilian part of their brains, the one based on fear and survival. Their choices were fight, flight, or freeze. In that moment, I wanted to be a leader and act from the more rational part of my brain. I figured the last thing Sweatshirt and Backward-Hat expected was a direct conversation, so I said, "Tell me more about that."

If I'm totally honest, I'd say my ego was getting the upper hand. I got sucked into the possibility that I might be able to change these dudes' minds. Or at least impress the students I was with. The two guys took me up on my invitation and came closer.

Sweatshirt Guy quoted Leviticus 18:22. "You shall not lie with a male as with a woman; it is an abomination," and I retorted with John 8:7, "Let any one of you who is without sin be the first to throw a stone." I had a few verses in my pocket thanks to an inclusive pastor I'd once heard speak. But we were both just trying to win the argument, not actually have a respectful dialogue. We were not searching for middle ground; we were searching for a definitive win. I am right, you are wrong, just admit it so we can move on.

"My mom taught me that when you set the table, everyone gets one spoon and one fork," said Sweatshirt Guy. "Never two spoons and no forks or vice versa."

I admit that I was lured into his analogy; I went into full tableware with him. "But, depending on the meal, you may run into a soupspoon or a salad fork," I quipped.

My expansion did not end our debate. He just kept going back to one spoon and one fork until things got personal.

"So, which one are you?" He looked intensely at me. It was no longer a moral argument. His tone made it feel like a personal attack. "A spoon or a fork?"

Now I felt that my very identity was in question. My primal fight, flight, or freeze hormones were raging. I went into full fight mode. I was stepping closer to him. I was gritting my teeth. Was I about to get into a physical confrontation with some guy I didn't know over an offhanded comment that I had decided to take on?

I knew how I wanted to behave. I wanted to stay calm and not get flustered. I wanted to communicate effectively and embody courage, grace, and empathy. I wanted to step up, and this was the perfect situation to do that. I did not want to be an agent of escalation.

But the rational part of my brain was drowned out by the reactive part. My face was red and I was clenching my fists. I knew I needed serotonin, but all I could feel was cortisol. My reptilian brain had taken over. The *Family Feud* buzzer was blasting in my ears. I couldn't reel in my reactivity, and I was as out of alignment as possible. There was nothing I could do about it. I knew what I needed to do, and I had even done it previously in similar interactions, but in that moment I could not get control of myself. I was not going to be a great model for these students.

Then Backward-Hat stepped in. He had been visibly rolling his eyes as his friend got more and more animated. It seemed that this wasn't the first time he'd been in an awkward situation with his buddy.

"Dude," he said to Sweatshirt Guy. "Some people are just sporks. He's a spork. Get over it."

I was so amped up that my first thought was, *Did you just call me "he"? And, why are we still talking about UTENSILS! You are obsessed with gender binaries. Have you never heard of chopsticks?!?*

But before I could unload, I heard Sweatshirt Guy say, "A spork, huh? Okay, I guess sporks are cool."

Now, I didn't really want to be thought of as a spork. I get it — I have a round face and spikey hair. But for a second it made sense to Sweatshirt Guy. It even made sense to me. There are a variety of problems with that analogy that range from inaccurate to offensive, but I got what he was saying. The reframe, coming from his friend, made him think about things differently. I ceased to be his enemy, and everyone calmed down. The guys walked away. The group of students I was with let out a sigh of relief. The confrontation was over. My cortisol and adrenaline simmered down, and the hormone scales tipped toward serotonin. I was moving back toward alignment.

I could have talked to Sweatshirt Guy until I was blue in the face and he likely would not have seen my point of view. I was so attached to being right, to winning the argument that I was not able to tap into my skills of stepping up. I was so caught up in trying to impress the students I was with that I couldn't strong-arm myself back into alignment. My reactivity eliminated any possible opportunity to connect with the guy. But Backward-Hat got through to his friend instantly. He knew exactly how to speak to his friend and be heard.

Obviously, I wish I'd handled the situation differently. If I could have simply taken deeper breaths, inserted a pause, and resisted mirroring his intensifying rage, I would have had a chance of being the leader I wanted to be. The fact that I couldn't locate any empathy for Sweatshirt Guy's perspective, find the humility to listen to his ideas without striving to win the argument, or tap into any patience inhibited me from being authentic. In that moment, I needed grace. I needed to see the higher purpose of that interaction and never lose sight of it. When the conversation escalated, I needed to not have escalated with it. If I could have taken the time to see it from his perspective, our ability to connect would have been infinitely greater, and our chance of reaching a more productive resolution would have increased. The fact that I was sucked into the conversation to the point of being ready to physically fight meant that I had lost sight of my higher purpose: I'd wanted to demonstrate to the students that although we don't need to avoid conflict, we must strive to remain our authentic selves in the face of such conflict.

As far as authenticity goes, there are other costs to being out of alignment. It takes a lot of time and energy to decide which version of ourselves we want to be in a given situation. In my situation, was I an activist? Was I an aggressor? Was I a victim? Was I a role model? What kind? Were all of those things mutually exclusive? Who was I? When we have to make either/or decisions about whether we will align with our internal self (our values) or our external self (our behaviors), we are in conflict with ourselves. We need to constantly decide which version of ourselves we are loyal to. What are the stakes and what are the repercussions? Who will we be in the moment?

As well, when we fall short of the expectations we have for ourselves, self-doubt starts to creep in. I started to wonder if I had lost the ability to be a leader. If I was triggered by one simple interaction, who was I to preach about inclusion? Was my hypocrisy as evident to everyone else as it was to me? The downward spiral of self-doubt is hard to bounce back from. From there, we can easily rationalize inaction. Why did I need to stand up to a bully? Why would I put myself in harm's way in any case? Inaction may be cowardly, but it is also safe. We are good at talking ourselves out of unknown, new, and different behaviors. If it ain't broke, why fix it—right?

Achieving authenticity is not something we accomplish and never think about again. It is completely normal to have self-doubt, but the critical action is to not jump ship. Falling down does not mean total failure. Failure only comes when we don't stand back up. We are committed to being everyday leaders, we must stay the course, even when the discomfort is with ourselves. We must recognize when we are out of alignment and recorrect ourselves.

Sometimes being out of alignment means we have internally changed who we want to be. There were plenty of times in my life when standing up to Sweatshirt Guy and even going to the point of physical altercation would have been authentic for me. Back then, I was in alignment when I was standing up for myself—no matter what the cost. But as I experienced more and more conflict, I changed who I wanted to be. Not because I wanted to back down but rather because I thought I could be more effective in shifting the perspective of people I came into contact with if I used kindness and compassion. Yelling and fighting no longer aligned with who I wanted to be. The action that previously felt authentic now made the *Family Feud* buzzers go off.

Humans are constantly evolving, so assessing and reassessing where we're at makes sense. What was authentic for me when I was ten years old is not necessarily authentic for me when I am forty. When I was ten, you couldn't drag me off of a sports field. I was intense and hypercompetitive. In gym class, I would steal the ball from the other kids on my own team so we would have a better chance of winning the game. I knew I was better than they were and could score. In retrospect, I see that I was a jerk. But that ten-year-old wanted to win. At everything. All the time. That is who I was on the inside. And my behavior matched that. Thirty-some years later, despite the fact that I still love to win, I no longer steal the ball from teammates. To be authentic in my forties, my behavior reflects who I strive to be—someone who values sportsmanship and teamwork. I strive to step up in all situations as much as I can. And when I can't, I learn from it.

There will always be external forces pushing us in different directions, so the only constant we have is our inner sense of authenticity. It is what roots us, grounds us, and allows us to be able to withstand those external storms. The practice of living authentically means incorporating all the skills we've covered in this book and using them skillfully and as flexibly as needed. Certain situations require a higher dose of one or more skills than others. The ability to apply the most appropriate skills at the best time and in the ideal proportion is what makes us everyday leaders.

Some of the pillars come easily to us, while others take a little more work. But as long as we are consciously striving to make decisions every day in which our actions align with our highest values, then we have the power to be the most impeccable version of ourselves. But it doesn't happen overnight. It isn't based on income or job title. It takes effort, and, most importantly, perseverance. We need to give ourselves time and permission to stumble. In reality, if we don't stumble, we are probably not challenging ourselves enough.

Our most transformational moments occur when we take the time to invoke one or more of the pillars, and act differently than we would have before. That consistent and intentional tweaking of actions to align with our best self is what makes us everyday leaders. Even if that self is a work in progress. In that sense, each one of our daily interactions has impact.

You are someone's inspiration. You have the power to live and act like the leader you are meant to be. And somewhere in your life, an opportunity to step up is happening right now. Don't miss it.

« Takeaways »

■ **Bring internal values into line with external behaviors.** To be authentic, we must first recognize the desires of our internal self. What are our values? Who do we aspire to be? Then we need to assess—with unsparing honesty—whether our external behaviors currently match those values. Where do we fall short? Where could we improve? What situations send us running into old, triggered behaviors? When we walk the talk—when our thinking and acting are in harmony—then we can actually be the person we strive to be.

- **Scan your body for signs of being out of alignment.** We know when we are in alignment. Our shoulders are back and our head is high. We feel comfortable and at ease. We are in integrity with ourselves. Alternatively, a sinking feeling in the pit of our stomach might indicate that our inner and outer selves are not in sync. Signs could be opening our mouth to speak but then holding back the words or feeling tense or uncomfortable somewhere in the body. Those sensations might indicate a need to reassess either ourselves or our situation.

- **Use the appropriate skill for the situation.** In order to live with authenticity, we need to get comfortable using the tools that will help us to navigate them in the most applicable way. Being able to assess the situation we are in and select the most appropriate tool or tools empowers us to be the best leader possible in the situation. This is a journey, so we will only learn what skill is appropriate when we try. We may choose the wrong skill to employ, but as long as we learn from the situation, we are growing.

- **Practice authenticity in low-stakes situations.** The time to put our authenticity to the test is not in high-stress situations. The higher the stakes, the harder it is to keep our cool and be authentic. It's much easier to practice when failure is irrelevant. Identify low-stakes situations in which to take risks and go for it.

⌃

STEP UP

Authenticity Challenge:
Set an Authenticity Goal

If we strive to be more authentic, we need to articulate what that looks like. First, identify situations in which you are not authentic — in certain places, among certain people, etc. Next, examine why you are not authentic in those situations. Is it fear, lack of confidence, lack of a role model, or something else? Now set a bold goal that would help you overcome the obstacle. What would be the first step in achieving that larger goal?

Here's an example. Let's say you are not authentic in certain meetings at work. Within your own department, you are outspoken and confident. But in companywide budget meetings, you don't speak up. You lack confidence because the whole financial process is confusing to you. Your bold goal may be emailing your boss to ask for a mentor to help you understand the financials better.

This simple act of sending the email to ask your boss for help comprises multiple pillars of leadership. First, it requires humility and courage to admit that you want help and to ask for it. It takes responsibility to do something about it. It takes grace to see the big picture. You have to be convinced that a greater understanding of the financial process is worth the fear that stems from appearing underqualified. You exhibit your individuality by showing the other strengths you bring to the table and patience by taking the time to learn something new as well as empathy for the issues that the financial team works with every day.

All of these things come together to empower you to be more authentic — you want to have a greater understanding of all facets of the business, but you know you can't achieve that on your own. This simple act of sending the email is a just one way of being an everyday leader. We all have situations in which we can practice authenticity. What is yours?

⌄

ACKNOWLEDGMENTS

This book would never have happened—and I would not be who I am—without the people below. Many, many thanks to the editorial folks at Sounds True. There are a lot of good people to thank, but I especially want to call out Editorial Director Haven Iverson for seeing this book long before I did and for circling back patiently and persistently until I was on board.

Thanks also to my editor and cocreator, Joelle Hann, for taking my incoherent thoughts and rambling stories and wrangling them into something other people can understand and enjoy, and thanks to Jade Lascelles, Chloe Prusiewicz, and Lindsey Kennedy at Sounds True. Also, thanks to Kelly Notaras for helping me navigate this wild world of publishing and ultimately land at Sounds True.

I got to this place of writing and publishing a book because of my speaking career—which came as a total surprise. I'm so glad it happened, because being an accidental advocate is exactly what I wanted to be when I grew up; I just didn't know it. For this, I have to thank Andrew Hyde and the TEDx Boulder and Ignite Boulder teams for giving me a chance to walk up on a stage and leave it all out there. You've changed the course of my life for the better, and I cannot thank you enough.

Also thanks to Adam Mordecai and the team at Upworthy, who singlehandedly made me viral. In a good way. Thank you for believing in my messages.

And thanks to Erin Weed for being an idea midwife. Your impact on my trajectory is immeasurable, and I'm very grateful for this.

Becoming an accidental advocate took some getting used to, including some insane feats of scheduling. Thanks to Gina Kirkland and Brian Regan for making sure I am in the right place at the right time and not working for free.

So many friends, colleagues, family members, and extended friend-family members make my life rich and remind me of what really matters. I couldn't do this without you. To Jennifer Brown, Nicole DeBoom, Sue Hellibronner, Wil Lewis, Cynthia Bowman, Andrew Plepler, Laura Witmer, Rae Stuart, Erin Uritus, Isabel Porras, Rachel Rubin — thank you for believing that I was ready for the big leagues before I did.

To Fred, Scott O., Adam, Sandy, Brian, Scott S., Suzanne, Kim, Sharon, Rachel, Ashley, Erica, Pamela, Kendal, Sunni, Katie O., Kelly, and all the other New Hopers past and present who helped me realize the joy and satisfaction of turning an empty building into a four-day spectacular.

To Dan Taylor, Kim Taylor, and Sandy Calvert, thanks for showing me that work doesn't have to feel like work.

To my Walnut Family, thanks for always giving me a soft place to land when I came home.

To Holly, Bob, Jeff, Sarah, Joey, Jack, Lynn, Katelyn, Chase, Leigh, Matt, Kathy and George, Susie and Dale, Pammy, Little Mand and Damon, Mike and Deb, Pat and Sue, Karen and Brian, Kelly and Cliff, Tami and Paul, Alice, Barb — thank you for always bringing your full selves to this wild and crazy family.

To Russell, Mollie, Tyler, Deborah, Angela, and Christian — thank you for welcoming me into your family with so much love.

To Gooy, Emily and Michael, Amy and Jaimi, Anna and Niki, Steph and Ang, Julia and Michael, Nicole, Meeks and Guthrie, Mara, Sarah and Sig, Barb and Megan, A, Skip and Nicolette, Mindy and Liz, Brock and Chelsea, Kayla and John, Amy and Chris, Taylor, Tyler, Kelly — thank you for the years, beers, and tears. Here's to treasuring more of all three. We are family, and I love you.

To Samantha, Addison, Lucy, Sam, Kennedy, Lane, Cade, Lila, Courtland, Grant, Summer, Evie, Jackson, Wyatt, Monroe, Benny, Grayson, Nova, Tallulah, Pyper, Dax, Hudson, Jack, Colyn, and all the little ones to come — thanks for letting me be "one of the kids." You inspire me to always find the fun, and you motivate us all to make the world a better place for you.

To Greg Rollet, thanks for being my eyes, my muscle, and my sounding board. But mostly thanks for always chatting about my dad.

To all my loved ones who have passed, thank you for blazing the trail. Even though you are out of sight, you are never out of mind.

Finally, to the central people in my day-to-day life, there's no way I can fully express my love and gratitude, but I'll try. Mom, thank you for teaching me what it means to be a strong woman. You have always been my biggest fan. To my sister, Mand, thank you for a lifetime of unconditional love and support and for never questioning when I wanted to be Danny. You will never know how much that meant to me.

Lacey, my wife, you are my anchor, my rock, my one. Thank you for encouraging my wild dreams and for keeping our life together while I pursue them. Your strength, selflessness, and steady hand amaze me daily. Thank you for saying yes. You have my whole heart, always.

To Luke, my son, thank you for inspiring me to be a better person each time I wake up. Of all the roles I have in life, my most cherished is being your mama.

ABOUT THE AUTHOR

Ash Beckham is an energetic and dynamic public speaker and author. Her online videos "I Am SO GAY" (Boulder Ignite), "Coming Out of Your Closet" (TEDx Boulder 2014) and "When to Take a Stand" (TEDx Boulder 2015) have garnered over 10 million views. By blending honesty and humor, Ash discusses everyday issues in an accessible and relatable way. Through a personal connection with her audience, Ash inspires people to step up to their full potential as leaders and be part of a bigger societal shift toward inclusion and equity. Ash challenges people to embrace the power of empathy, respect, and hard conversations.

Ash lives in Longmont, Colorado with her amazing wife Lacey, their incredible son Luke, and their cantankerous dog Grizzly.

For more, visit ashbeckham.com.

ABOUT SOUNDS TRUE

Sounds True is a multimedia publisher whose mission is to inspire and support personal transformation and spiritual awakening. Founded in 1985 and located in Boulder, Colorado, we work with many of the leading spiritual teachers, thinkers, healers, and visionary artists of our time. We strive with every title to preserve the essential "living wisdom" of the author or artist. It is our goal to create products that not only provide information to a reader or listener but also embody the quality of a wisdom transmission.

For those seeking genuine transformation, Sounds True is your trusted partner. At SoundsTrue.com you will find a wealth of free resources to support your journey, including exclusive weekly audio interviews, free downloads, interactive learning tools, and other special savings on all our titles.

To learn more, please visit SoundsTrue.com/freegifts or call us toll-free at 800.333.9185.

In loving memory of Beth Skelley, book designer extraordinaire.
Her spirit lives on in our books and in our hearts.